THE NEXT GENERATION
OF WOMEN LEADERS

THE NEXT GENERATION OF WOMEN LEADERS

WHAT YOU NEED TO LEAD BUT WON'T LEARN IN BUSINESS SCHOOL

Selena Rezvani

Foreword by
Gail Evans

PRAEGER

An Imprint of ABC-CLIO, LLC

Santa Barbara, California • Denver, Colorado • Oxford, England

Library of Congress Cataloging-in-Publication Data

Rezvani, Selena.
  The next generation of women leaders : what you need to lead but won't learn in business school /
Selena Rezvani.
     p. cm.
  Includes bibliographical references and index.
  ISBN 978-0-313-37666-5 (hbk. : alk. paper) — ISBN 978-0-313-37667-2 (ebook)
  1. Women executives. 2. Leadership in women. 3. Success in business. 4. Generation X. 5. Genera-
tion Y. I. Title.
  HD6054.3.R49 2009
  658.4'092082—dc22   2009039703

14 13 12 11 10   1 2 3 4 5

This book is also available on the World Wide Web as an eBook.
Visit www.abc-clio.com for details.

Praeger
An Imprint of ABC-CLIO, LLC

ABC-CLIO, LLC
130 Cremona Drive, P.O. Box 1911
Santa Barbara, California 93116-1911

This book is printed on acid-free paper ∞

Manufactured in the United States of America

For my nephews, Alexander, Omar,
Cyrus, Ali, and Maxim,
in the hope that they will grow up in a
world whose leaders represent all of our voices

CONTENTS

Acknowledgments

Heartfelt Thanks:

To my husband Geoff, my cornerstone: Thank you for believing in me the way you do. Through your words and actions, you have taught me the meaning of unconditional love and support.

To my father and mother, Noor and Genevieve Khan: I am blessed to be the recipient of your encouragement, love, and guidance. Thank you for always insisting that I find a career that I love. I have! Your belief in me gave me what I needed to pull this off.

To the Rezvanis: I thank you for welcoming me into your wonderful family, treating me like your own, and rallying behind my dreams.

To my three siblings, Yasmin, Anisa, and Shazad: So much of what I have learned over the years has been shaped by being your "little" sister. I am so grateful to you. A little bit of each of your leadership styles can be found intertwined in these pages.

To Peggy Ann Schmitt, a beautiful woman leader who the world lost to cancer this year: Thank you for being an incredible role model. Your vivacious, loving, and generous spirit lives on in the myriad of people who got to learn from you.

To the strong, talented legion of women that I get to call my girlfriends: You had a major hand in making this book possible. Thank you for thinking I could do it.

To the faculty and students of the Johns Hopkins MBA Fellows program (second cohort): Your encouragement and ideas helped this book go from idea to reality. I value your friendship and all that you have taught me about leadership over the last two years.

To Jeff Olson, the acquisitions editor who took a chance on my idea and enthusiastically supported me: Jeff, your open-mindedness and patience mean the world to me.

Finally, to the 30 women whose insights and advice formed the foundation of this book: you have my deepest respect and gratitude. You have inspired me and indelibly changed how I see the world of leadership. I hope you find a deep sense of satisfaction in knowing how many women you will help.

FOREWORD

Finally a book that advances the leadership outlook for Generation X and Y women. At last, ambitious younger women can learn about the characteristics that have best served women executives, and yet hear advice that is targeted to Generation X and Y's specific age and life experience level.

The combination of stories, advice, and theory presented in the following pages exemplifies the power of women helping other women, the most important power we have.

Additionally, the book emphasizes ownership over your own career. Ultimately we are responsible for our own success. Selena Rezvani contends that finding your passion and seeking a career that matches your values are two of the central tasks of leadership development. She argues compellingly that a woman must see leadership opportunities and strategize to achieve her goals. Young women must see their careers long-range, avoiding the more passive approach of shifting from job to job.

Further, this book helps us to see an important confluence of events; women have never been readier to lead, and the global workplace now demands their unique competencies more than ever. Undeniably, one of the book's best contributions is the section explaining that women who can promote themselves and comfortably ask for what they want are more likely to move into leadership. These and other empowering concepts are richly illustrated through the stories and advice of women at top echelons of their fields.

Whether you approach the issue of leadership development as a student, a new professional, a seasoned worker, an employer, or anyone else wanting to attain success, this innovative book adds a new dimension to leadership development literature. The value a reader will derive can help them improve personally, but even better: I believe a reader's newfound knowledge will have a cascading effect. Readers will be encouraged to pull other women up! As you read this book, remember, for every woman who succeeds, all women succeed. For every woman who fails, all women fail. Now is the time to help each other to be successful. Go for it!

Gail Evans
Author, *Play Like a Man, Win Like a Woman* and
Executive Vice President, CNN Newsgroup (retired)

INTRODUCTION

As a first year MBA student and aspiring executive, I was extremely disheartened to learn of the low number of women leaders in business. When I looked upward, I saw few executives I could relate to in charge of the visible, important businesses I studied in school. Furthermore, the research I started to do confirmed that what I thought was a low representation of women executives in the United States was in fact a dismal representation.

I wanted to learn more. I sought out—and devoured—books detailing how women had made it to the top of organizations. With a voracious appetite for this material, I wanted to understand what traits or career strategies "the elusive few" had in common that helped them achieve their status. While I gleaned considerable insights from the books I read, the advice provided was targeted at no particular age or experience level of an aspiring woman leader. This meant that as a 30-year-old professional, I was getting the same advice as a 65-year-old, much more seasoned and experienced reader. I wanted more precise advice, focused specifically on Generation X and Y women like me.

As disheartened as I was by the figures that I read, I was simultaneously deeply motivated to do something about it. In 2008, propelled by my curiosity and hunger for knowledge, I seized an independent study opportunity in my MBA program as a means to access these women and start a dialogue.

I researched high-ranking women in various industries and identified a list of professionals from different backgrounds and job roles, with different degrees. While I faced the challenge of not personally knowing any members of this group, I decided to appeal to them anyway, with a request for a meeting. I wanted to have conversations with women who led family businesses, Fortune 500 companies, nonprofit organizations, and who served as important officials in our government. I drafted my "dream list" of interviewees and made contact with them one by one. I explained to each executive my vision for gleaning their hardest-won lessons and advice and sharing them with other young women. To my amazement, more and more executives said yes to interviews, and the momentum built.

Beginning in January of 2008, I conducted interviews with 30 women CEOs, CFOs, COOs, chairs, presidents, and executive vice presidents. The interviews yielded invaluable insights into the professional lives of women. I asked questions related to how Generation X and Y women should approach career advancement. I asked about managing subordinates, using influence, developing a presence, negotiating on the job, and methods for augmenting credibility, among others. My primary intention was to find out what women leaders wished they had known earlier in their careers and what knowledge was most essential to their advancement. The advice shared in the interviews uncovered vitally important career practices for young women. Regardless of interviewee context—whether entrepreneurs, officers of Fortune 500 companies, or high-ranking officials in government—clear themes emerged from the interviews. These themes appear as Chapters 2–9 of this book, and I hope you will benefit from their contents as much as I have.

The advice the interviewees provided had a major impact on me, so much so, in fact, that I found myself doing and seeing things differently immediately afterward. In one situation, I left a morning interview galvanized by what I had heard and set up an afternoon meeting with my boss in which I asked for a substantial raise—a "bump up" that I was later granted. After another interview, I became keenly aware of how often I apologized unnecessarily or diminished the strength of my ideas with statements like, "I'm not sure if this is a good idea but . . ." or "This might be a null point but . . ." Following yet another interview, I went to my performance review armed and ready as a full participant rather than a passive listener. I brought with me substantiation of my best contributions: accolades I had received and initiatives I had spearheaded over the previous year. Perhaps the biggest change was a mental shift. I became the chief executive—and chief decision maker—of my own career and advancement. Rather than sitting on the sidelines wondering what kind of career would "happen to me," I now see that each of us needs to own every one of our past successes and nurture every future aspiration that we have. As you take in the advice and numerous strategies in this book, expect to reap two equally important, but simple benefits: you will have more tools to propel your career forward and fewer limitations on what you think is possible.

1

HOW FAR HAVE WE COME?

THE SCOPE OF THE ISSUES

Why write a book on women and leadership? If women make up roughly half of the workforce, have we not progressed enough as a society? After all, one would think the "glass ceiling" has shattered by now. While there is a pervading perception that men and women have achieved generally equal status in the U.S. workplace, statistics tell another story. Women lag significantly behind men in terms of pay and in the representation of the leadership of our businesses, government agencies, boards, and political systems. The reality is that we are not "there" yet.

Statistics of female leaders are moving in the right direction, but slowly. Catalyst, a nonprofit organization that works with businesses to build inclusive workplaces and expand opportunities for women, found through its report, *Catalyst Pyramid: U.S. Women in Business,* that women make up 46.5% of the total U.S. workforce, and yet only 15.7% of women are employed as corporate officers with Fortune 500 companies. This figure has changed little from previous years when 15.7% (2008) and 15.4% (2007) of corporate officer positions were held by women. More dramatic still, women make up only 3% of chief executive officers in Fortune 500 companies (Catalyst, 2009).

The same report found that women's representation on the boards of Fortune 500 companies is also slow to improve. In 2008 women made up 15.2% of the membership of Fortune 500 boards, up only slightly from 14.8% in 2007. Assuming a similar yearly growth rate of 0.4% continued, women could expect equal representation on Fortune 500 boards in the year 2095. Catalyst President Ilene H. Lang noted that a passive approach to diversity can hurt a company's performance. She stated, "Increased globalization and shifting demographics dictate that diversity and the advancement of women on corporate boards are strategic business imperatives that twenty-first century companies cannot afford to ignore" (Catalyst, 2005).

When you consider how women compare to men from an educational standpoint, women now earn more than one-half of all bachelor and master's degrees in the United States, and nearly one-half of all doctoral degrees (National Center for Education Statistics, 2007). Furthermore, a positive trend exists where women now make up close to half of medical and law school graduates. In a 2008 article in The Wall Street Journal by Sue Shellenbarger, the author notes that female enrollment at full-time MBA programs has remained flat at 30%, while the figures trend up to 49% in medical schools and 47% in law schools. Even though statistics representing women are more favorable than ever in law and medicine, closer examination of research shows us that careers in these fields do not necessarily retain women. In its report *Women in Law*, Catalyst found, for example, that over the 2006–2007 academic year, women made up 46.7% of law school students, 34.4% of all lawyers, and only 18.7% of all partners. The thinning effect, as a woman in law moves upward, tells us that the career path to leadership is less accessible or attractive to women, or perhaps incompatible with their lives.

WHAT DOES IT ALL MEAN?

The fact that there are few women in top roles has a series of effects. For one, there are fewer visible female leaders for younger women to emulate. With few role models to look up to, young women have less access to and opportunity for dialogue with female leaders, including women executives' most important lessons learned and advice. Perhaps most destructive, if a woman looks upward and sees few or no leaders she can relate to, she may never see leadership as a believable future for her or other women.

BARRIERS

Numerous women I interviewed cited the importance of understanding the barriers to leadership that still exist. These roadblocks were mentioned not to discourage aspiring women leaders, but to arm them with important information that could help them circumnavigate the obstacles. Barriers for women who want to lead can be social, economic, psychological—even generational. The better we understand them, the better we can manage creatively around these impediments. As Rosslyn Kleeman, Chair of the Coalition for Effective Change, astutely noted, "There is a mistaken idea that barriers no longer exist, but there are still a lot. . . . Women need to find a happy medium between acknowledging the barriers that exist and forging ahead anyway."

SOCIAL BARRIERS

Socially we are getting increasingly accustomed to seeing women in management and leadership positions. However, because of many men and women's early social conditioning, some simply cannot get used to the idea of a woman as a credible leader in the workplace. Often women are criticized if they are perceived as being too feminine or too masculine in their leadership style. Further, messages we received early on that women are not natural "leadership material" or are better suited to "help" rather than "lead" are untrue and unhelpful.

Consider these studies as you understand some of the representative social barriers that women face:

- In a state university study, course syllabi were distributed to 141 students. The students were asked to review the syllabi of courses which were taught by men and women and represented a variety of course topics, including one course called Sociology of Gender. The students were then asked to rate the syllabi according to a number of questions. When evaluating the Sociology of Gender syllabus taught by a female instructor, students were more likely to indicate that the course topics appeared overly political, biased, and contained subjective exams and papers. Across the study population of men and women, a bias emerged against the female instructor of the course, which was strongest among male students. When a male professor's name was listed on the same exact course syllabus, ratings given were more positive. Specifically students rated the male instructor more favorably in terms of assigning reasonable work, being credible and available to students, and having less bias. The study showed that when the same exact course was taught by a man versus a woman, the course was considered more appealing and more comprehensive (Moore & Trahan, 1997).
- Another study, conducted by Julie E. Phelan, Corinne A. Moss-Racusin, and Laurie A. Rudman of Rutgers University, compared perceptions of men and women who interviewed for the same job. A male and female pair of actors was coached and instructed to display behaviors in a job interview associated with agentic or "masculine" qualities, like aggression and ambition. The actors were then taped while interviewing for a job. Study participants were asked to watch the tape and appraise the job applicants' competence, social skills, and hire-ability. The women interviewees who presented themselves agentically were evaluated as competent but lacking social skills, which ultimately hurt their hire-ability. By contrast, confident and

ambitious male candidates were evaluated as competent, likable, and were more likely to be hired than a woman with similar traits (Phelan, Moss-Racusin, & Rudman, 2008).

As you consider the findings of these studies, and the preponderance of similar ones, you can understand some of the nuanced social barriers women face as leaders. Whether they are leading a classroom or interviewing to be a leader—as the cases above illustrate—women are often not seen as intellectually or emotionally equipped as their male counterparts. Stereotypes of women as too passive, too emotional, or too unambitious to lead are simply not based in reality. I provided the illustrative examples of discrimination above to raise your awareness of such dynamics in your own workplace. If and when you feel that you or your ideas are being discounted wrongfully at work, remember some of the dynamics of social conditioning, and that they may be playing a role in your situation.

WOMEN VERSUS WOMEN: REALLY?

Some of the women I interviewed, and some of the studies I researched, talked about barriers that women impose on other women. Specifically this manifested in interviews as a pattern where women at the top, or those vying for a leadership role, compete with one another rather than help each other. Vicki Ho, General Manager, Asia Services for GE Healthcare Clinical Services at General Electric, shared her own observation of this occurrence noting, "Women will not necessarily pull other women up with them when they get promoted. Someone who's broken open the doors to the senior level may still feel threatened by other women." She added, "The higher up you go, the more qualified people there are with like skills to your own. Some people react by cutting others down."

Similarly, Mei Xu, Founder and Chief Executive Officer of Chesapeake Bay Candle, Blissliving Home, commented on this workplace barrier, sharing, "It is not only men who may sometimes have issues with a woman business leader—sometimes it is also women. I don't know exactly why but it seems that some women can be afraid of other women who are successful or smart."

As disheartening as this dynamic is, some interviewees noted a lessening effect of woman-versus-woman friction at work. DeeDee Wilson, Chief Financial Officer at Aritzia, recalled, "When I was first starting out in business, one barrier was other women. Perhaps because there were so few jobs at the top, women were very competitive with one another. However, in the last 7–10 years, women in the work force seem to understand that it is in everyone's best interest for women to support each other."

Ultimately female executives can present a wonderful resource to younger and less experienced women. We all benefit when the leadership of our organizations is representative of the combined male and female workforce, and it helps to remember that there is enough "room for everyone" and countless leadership opportunities all around us.

ECONOMIC PARITY

Economics present a different kind of obstacle for women. Naomi C. Earp, Chair of the Equal Employment Opportunity Commission, reiterated this point, sharing in our interview, "One barrier is around pay equity—data shows that women make about 80% of what men do." The Institute for Women's Policy Research found the ratio of women's to men's median weekly earnings for full-time workers to be 79.9% in 2008, the third consecutive decline since the historical high of 81% in 2005 (Institute for Women's Policy Research, 2009). If a woman thinks she will not be paid fairly for equal work, she may be discouraged from becoming an executive, or dismiss it altogether as a worthwhile career path.

Nonetheless, the Equal Pay Act of 1963 prohibits sex-based wage discrimination between men and women in the same establishment who perform jobs that require equal skill, effort, and responsibility (The U.S. Equal Employment Opportunity Commission). More recently President Obama signed the Lilly Ledbetter Fair Pay Act of 2009, which makes it easier to file a compensation discrimination charge (Open Congress, 2009). Additionally, further momentum has been harnessed with the Paycheck Fairness Act, which has already passed the House and is now pending in the Senate. According to the National Women's Law Center, this additional piece of legislation could serve to strengthen our current laws against wage discrimination and provide tools to enable the federal government to be more proactive in preventing wage discrimination.

To fight the barrier of wage disparity, a nonprofit organization called The WAGE Project, which does admirable work to close the wage gap between men and women, was formed by Evelyn Murphy. WAGE Clubs have been formed nationally where women can come together for personal support and help each other take action individually and collectively to help close the wage gap. I suggest young women in particular get involved in The WAGE Project as a means to learn about their own possible wage gap; what it means now, in the future, and in retirement years.

PSYCHOLOGICAL IMPEDIMENTS

Lastly psychological barriers get in the way of our leadership potential when we disqualify ourselves from opportunities. Even if our viewpoint lacks supporting evidence, our own psychological barriers may tell us things like, "I could never do a job with a heavy finance component," "I couldn't lead others successfully because no one would listen to me," or "I won't be promoted even if I apply for the job."

Jeanine Becker, Senior Counsel at Motorola, Inc., commented on this phenomenon when she reflected, "[One] barrier is that women don't always think they have the capability to lead. I often hear women colleagues say, 'I need one more year in my job in order to be ready for that opportunity,' or 'If that job opportunity came up in 2–3 years, I would take it.' Women feel a need for a certain level of prior training and experience that men do not necessarily demand in order to jump into a new role. There's a need for women to trust themselves more and ask themselves, 'What resources would it take for me to be comfortable *enough* to succeed with this step up in responsibility?' Can the organization provide coaching, mentoring, training, or something else to facilitate my success?" Clearly, getting comfortable with and even embracing a certain level of risk is an important hallmark of a leader.

Being young can intensify these self-imposed psychological barriers because we can lack the benefit of years of experience and deep confidence in our professional abilities. Donna Callejon, Chief Operating Officer at GlobalGiving, shared her own observation of this trend when she noted, "A young woman's own ambivalence can create a psychological barrier. I regularly see a pattern of younger women who are not sure what they want to do and are afraid to take a wrong step. They seem to think if they screw up, they won't be able to bounce back." Have you ever disqualified yourself from an interesting assignment you wanted to pursue? Have you talked yourself out of taking a risk? Do you have regrets about opting out of an opportunity?

The beauty of being young is that our careers have resilience. We do not need to see decisions or career risks as "all or nothing." Additionally the barriers and limitations that we impose on ourselves are one of the few obstacles over which *we* have control. Consider what, if any, psychological barriers you carry around; think about if they have ever served you in a positive way (my guess is not), and then let them go!

THE BUSINESS CASE FOR DIVERSITY

Despite some of the barriers to leadership that women face, there is a compelling case to be made for diversity. Taking an inclusive approach to the management teams of our organizations (as well as the leadership of our political system, religious groups, boards, and government agencies) is first and foremost the right thing to do. Further, considerable data shows that a diverse workforce benefits everyone. Supporting this thinking, DeeDee Wilson of Aritzia told me, "There is also more recognition by men that there is a strong business case for diversity, that it's not just some government initiative. . . . I think in today's business world there is more value placed on the ability to use both intuition and analytics. Many women naturally have this capability and if they learn to use it early in their career, it can be an advantage for them."

Another powerful benefit of an inclusive culture is that it allows people to bring their whole "selves" to work, which can often lead to enhanced creativity, problem solving, and innovation for a company. Strong diversity management helps employees to feel they can venture a risk and contribute their greatest strengths. An additional strength of effective diversity initiatives is that they help organizations retain employees—and customers— who are increasingly discriminating in terms of where they want to spend their energy and dollars. Furthermore, many organizations have demonstrated how those companies recognized for being inclusive workplaces are also more profitable. DiversityInc, for example, conducted a study showing that over a 10-year period, the publicly traded companies in its Top 50 Companies for Diversity Index yielded as much as 23.5 percent higher returns than the Standard & Poor's 500 over a 10-year period with dividends reinvested (DeGroat, 2006).

WOMENOMICS

Yet another reason for more organizations to take an inclusive approach with their leadership teams has to do with consumer trends. A commonly cited statistic tells us that women make an astounding 83% of all consumer purchases. Tom Peters' book *Re-Imagine! Business Excellence in a Disruptive Age* highlights the influence women have on current household purchases as well as our future economy noting, "In category after category, women are instigators-in-chief of most consumer purchases." An additional business reason for including women in important leadership roles, therefore, is that they have tremendous insight into the ever-important consumer. To truly lead your competition in industries such as consumer products, it is a requirement to have leaders who represent the customer population.

While there are still some people who do not understand or who do not buy into the concept of diversity, one thing is clear—as a global workforce entrenched in tough economic times, we need everyone's intelligence more than ever. Patricia Deyton, Director of the Center for Gender in Organizations at Simmons School of Management reinforced this point when she said,

"There's a changing climate driven by progress over the past few decades. There is the realization that women, who make up half of the population, have just as much to contribute as men. There's also a greater understanding that we need to use everyone's intelligence; that there is strength in a diverse workforce." Women have much to contribute and including them in leadership has limitless positive benefits for many stakeholders.

THE NEXT GENERATION OF WOMEN LEADERS

As more doors open for women, my belief is that the leadership landscape will continue to progress from a gender perspective. One major reason is that women's natural leadership style—which differs from that of men—is a perfect complement to the talent needs of the new economic era we are entering. Economic, global, generational, and technological changes require a leader with a mix of hard and soft skills, and women's natural propensity in these areas makes them ideal business leaders. More and more research substantiates that contrary to outmoded, archaic thinking, women are well prepared to lead in the twenty-first century.

Certainly critical thinking and problem solving are needed in a global work environment that is moving at a faster pace than ever. Thoughtful planning underpins good critical thinking and problem-solving skills, as evidenced in a recent study by Merrill Lynch entitled *When It Comes to Investing, Gender a Strong Influence on Behavior*. Among other findings, the study showed that women were less likely than men to hold onto a losing investment too long, less likely to allocate too much money to one investment, and less likely to buy a "trendy" or popular stock without first doing research. Women's ability to plan carefully was considered a key reason they outperformed men in the study.

Women's comfort with collaboration, including turning to others when they do not have certain knowledge, was also credited in women outperforming men in the study. Robert C. Doll, Jr., president and chief investment officer of Merrill Lynch Investment Managers noted, "In gender terms, the survey found that a little self-knowledge can go a long way. Women know what they don't know and aren't afraid to ask for help, turning to professional financial advisors at a much greater rate than men" (Merrill Lynch, 2005). By not expecting ourselves to have all the expertise all the time, we can reach out for input and effectively resolve issues.

Women's ability to multitask and to build consensus are two other traits that are increasingly needed in a global, complex work environment where virtual interactions and relationships are commonplace. Having long been expected to work outside the home and act as heads of households, women are constantly juggling priorities and resolving conflict. Supporting this idea was Mei Xu of Chesapeake Bay Candle, Blissliving Home, who noted, "Women are naturally great multitaskers. Women also have a strong moral compass. . . . We're not conflict inducers, we're conflict resolvers. And it's not that women can't 'do' conflict, they just prefer situations where everyone wins." Entrepreneurial skill is another badly needed competency in the new economy. Women find themselves in situations all the time where they must make decisions with limited information. Inspirational leadership, team building, and decisiveness are just some of the characteristics that make women equipped to take an entrepreneurial approach to business.

Finally women are naturals at communication and relationship building. Advanced skills are required in these areas when working with employees and customers from disparate cultures, backgrounds, religions, and customs, and women thrive in creating a true two-way exchange in relationships. According to Judy B. Rosener, author of *America's Competitive Secret: Women Managers,* "Women speak and hear a language of connection and intimacy, and men speak and hear a language of status and independence. Men communicate to obtain information, establish their status, and show independence. Women communicate to create relationships, encourage interaction, and exchange feelings" (Rosener, 1997).

Further supporting women's natural leadership abilities is Lawrence A. Pfaff, EdD, a human resources consultant who conducted a study released in 2001 of 2,482 managers at all levels, from more than 400 organizations across 19 states. Dr. Pfaff found that female managers scored higher than their male counterparts in 20 different skill areas. He noted, "Female managers—as rated by their bosses, themselves and the people who work for them—were rated significantly better than their male counterparts. This difference extends beyond the 'softer' skills such as communication, feedback and empowerment to such areas as decisiveness, planning and setting standards" (American Psychological Association, 1999).

TIME FOR A NEW KIND OF LEADER

Women, and young women in particular, are ready to take the leadership reins. The tools outlined in the chapters that follow will help you to comprehensively manage your career advancement, including the path you choose to take in becoming a leader. The chapters flow in a way that corresponds to how we experience work: preparing for and finding the right job, engaging in value-added on-the-job and off-the-job activities, and building a powerful network. I also address the art of asking for what you want, navigating office politics, managing work and personal realms, and planning for your career in a long-term way.

Positioning Yourself to Lead

FIRST, LOCATE YOUR PASSION

If you only remember one thing from this book, the key to leveraging your strengths and leadership abilities lies in having a career that feeds your passion. As many of the women I interviewed pointed out, perks or sizeable salaries do not necessarily lead to professional happiness. Instead, finding passion and meaning in your work builds the foundation of a successful career trajectory. Furthermore, a career with meaning aligns with your values and fulfills you on a more consistent basis than jobs with prestige alone. Jeanine Becker, Senior Counsel at Motorola, Inc., however, points out that passion is not a fixed target; shifts are to be expected. She advised, "View your career as an adventure. . . . Realize that you can learn from every job and that the perfect job for you is going to change over time. . . . Let things evolve and be willing to take a leap." All too often we underestimate or completely overlook passion in the pursuit of career advancement.

PASSION LEADS TO ENGAGEMENT

Research shows that passion and meaning in one's work leads to increased engagement. If you are passionate about your work, you are more likely to exhibit the traits of an engaged employee. I particularly like how the Institute for Employment Studies defines this phenomenon, that engagement is "a positive attitude held by the employee towards the organization and its values. An engaged employee is aware of business context, and works with colleagues to improve performance within the job for the benefit of the organization" (Robinson et al., 2004). Moreover, Gallup, the research consultancy that conducted numerous pioneering studies on employee engagement, found that passionate workers are the most likely to create value for their employers. They note that "engaged employees work with passion and feel a profound connection to their company. They drive innovation and move the organization forward" (Gallup Management Journal, 2006).

Being "engaged" means that when faced with the choice to volunteer your discretionary effort to a project or work task, chances are you will. Quite simply, engaged employees more often go the extra mile. Ultimately, finding a career you love will make you a harder worker, better at what you do, and will reap significant dividends for your company. While there is likely to be more than one career path to which you are well suited, the hardest task for many young women is to identify one viable career path.

This chapter sheds light on exercises and tools that can help you tap into your passion and find meaning at work. While women today have tremendous choice in terms of the industry and position they pursue, taking the time to strategize about a passion-driven career is a worthy investment of your time and energy. No matter how you engage in this process of self-discovery, I encourage you to think without limiting yourself and to be open to what you find. You may discover that your passion centers on a particular function, role, industry group, location, or even a set of values. Alternatively, you may find your passion indirectly by bumping into a certain role or job, or through the process of eliminating jobs that are not right for you.

IT'S ALL ABOUT YOU

Numerous people—men and women alike—are struck by how personal the process of career exploration can be. Why? Because career choices are ones we make based on a variety of personal factors including our upbringing, interests, skills, and training. Our career decisions are also shaped by our self-esteem, academic experiences, financial circumstances, tolerance for risk, and many other dynamics. Is it any wonder then, that our career aspirations, struggles, and successes are deeply personal? You simply cannot separate "you" from your career.

The women I interviewed showed an openness to the process of self-discovery and continually ask themselves if their career aligns with their deepest held needs and values. Leading, they found, requires having the courage to pursue what you truly want without making choices to appease others. The closer you can maneuver to what you *really* want to do, they conveyed, the more confidence you will gain in your decisions and the more others' expectations will simply fall away. Naomi C. Earp, Chair of the U.S. Equal Employment Opportunity Commission, reiterated this point sharing, "We need to know what we're really good at and figure out what we love, what gives us pleasure. I was told to go into bankruptcy law because there were few women and few blacks in the field. Once I actually tried it, I almost died! It's important to do something that you feel is enjoyable and fun. Don't let people overlay their own career expectations on you. Do something that you, specifically, enjoy."

SUSTAIN YOURSELF WITH MEANING

If passion is going to position you for success, then your passion needs to come from an authentic place. We are not all nurses, charity workers, or human rights lawyers by day, but we can still find work that sustains us personally. So how do we still find a sense of meaning in what we do?

Consider these examples of everyday women finding meaning in their work:

- Aisha J., a freelance CPA and accountant—"I've always been a 'rules' kind of person. I prefer structure to open-ended assignments. With accounting, I get to help people through the convoluted process of filling out tax forms. Many times, because of my expertise, I save them hundreds of dollars."
- Zoe C., an advertising executive at a consumer products company— "The mix of creativity, people skills, and business savvy in advertising is my perfect complement. I won't move into a different role, even though I've had offers. What I love about my job is helping people clarify their message. I help them express it effectively."
- Sarah P., a broker at a large mortgage house—"I found that I love working in this industry. In many cases, I am helping people secure their very first home. I go home every night knowing that I've made peoples' dreams come true."
- Daniella V., a marketing coordinator at an IT company—"I've discovered my niche working for innovative IT companies. What we do makes information accessible to the world. Plus, my personal values are pretty similar to those that the company stands for. I know that no matter what other jobs I pursue, they will have to be with cutting-edge, future-focused companies like this one."

Finding personal meaning in your work can happen in many forms, as the examples above illustrate. Aisha enjoys the structured nature of accounting and is motivated by the challenge of saving people money. Zoe, however, is enthralled with the larger landscape of her industry. The field of advertising keeps Zoe on her toes and demands the type of skills that she wants to use and hone on a day-to-day basis. Sarah, in contrast, finds that working for a company that offers mortgages to prospective homeowners allows her to play a positive role in peoples' lives. In yet another perspective, Daniella found that her true preference is working for forward-thinking companies whose values match her own. Daniella has discovered that she is not necessarily tied to a specific company, but rather a specific *type* of company. You may have noticed that each of these women mentioned that they help people in some way through their work. While it may not appear to most of us on the surface that these women are in "helping" professions, they have each chosen to view their jobs from a lens that makes it personally meaningful.

Your personal values play a significant role in helping you make smart career choices. Catherine J. Mathis, Senior Vice President of Corporate Communications at The New York Times Company, stressed the importance of this practice. She noted, "I found a workplace that mirrors my values. I love our company and the media business. When you find a place that fits your values, you will naturally be more successful. Working for The New York Times Company has brought out abilities in me I didn't know I had." Similarly, Katharine Weymouth, Publisher of the *Washington Post* and Chief Executive Officer of Washington Post Media, noted, "I feel strongly that a reliable news-generating entity is a critical component of democracy. I'd like to be remembered for taking that entity and making it better than when I originally got it." Regardless of what job you hold, find a way to see how your contribution makes a positive impact. The questions below are intended to stimulate your thinking around pride and meaning. Ask yourself these questions as you think through the impact you make:

- What do you do in your role that makes a difference in your organization?
- What do you do in your role that makes a difference in your broader industry?
- What do you do in your role that makes a difference in society as a whole?
- How does your work help people?
- What do you take particular pride in doing at work?

TYING YOUR CAREER TO YOUR VALUES

In my own experience consulting to companies about how to become better workplaces, I have discovered the depth of one of my own core values. I have found that I need to work for an organization whose employees are a priority. Whether that means employees are valued and developed professionally, consulted on matters that affect them, or treated in a humanistic fashion, people have to matter. It is one of my most deeply held values that if you treat people the way they like to be treated, you will create trusting, lasting, and highly productive relationships. This has certainly shaped the direction and focal point of my work, and has allowed me to find a career where I have made a positive impact. As a management consultant, I have interviewed and surveyed thousands of employees who have not always had a voice at their company. If you can see how your work matters, you will excel at your job, and I promise you, people around you will take notice.

USING SELF-ASSESSMENTS TO LIGHT THE WAY

Many young women I have known want to find a career they are passionate about, and yet cannot pinpoint where their particular interests lie. Self-assessments can certainly shed light on what makes you tick in a way that can quickly "cut through the fog." Specifically, self-assessments can provide insights that lead to identifying your preferred industry, job role, or, at the very least, providing information of your dominant traits or work style.

In my experience, assessments provide information that is confirmatory—that is, it substantiates patterns of which you are already aware. In my own life these assessments have reinforced the career path I have chosen and have helped give me confidence in my next step. For example, career assessments usually paint a similar picture of me; they illustrate that I am a strong fit for fields like consulting, psychology, and business, where I can problem-solve one-on-one with people and teams. Similarly, personality-focused assessments tell me that I prefer people to things, and rely on feelings and intuition more often than data and facts. Why do such results matter? Quite simply, when you find a career that leverages your dominant personality traits, preferences, and career interests, work is not a chore or bother, rather it feels natural and effortless. Assessments also give you a confidence boost by reinforcing what you may have long suspected, but for which you did not necessarily have outside validation.

An important aspect of self-assessments is learning about your preferences. An assessment may highlight that one woman prefers structured, rule-bound work environments, which may be best suited in a role like accounting, for example. Alternatively, an assessment may show another individual's tendency toward ambiguous, nonstructured settings, as is the case for sales people and recruiters, among others. Knowing what settings and environments you gravitate toward can give you a level of comfort on the job that allows you to quickly "hit the ground running" and be highly effective.

WHAT ARE YOUR PREVAILING PREFERENCES AND HOW DO THEY SHAPE YOUR CHOICES?

The list of assessments in Table 2.1 covers areas such as personality and psychological type, career and interest, skill, and values. The list notes the area the assessment focuses on, if it requires professional interpretation services or is "self-directed," and whether a fee, if any, is charged.

Table 2.1   Self-Assessments

Assessment	Area of Focus	Requires Professional Interpretation	Fee
Personality and Psychological Type			
DiSC® Assessment	Behavioral Styles and Preferences	Yes	Fee
Fundamental Interpersonal Relations Orientation-Behavior™ (FIRO-B®)	Interpersonal Relations	Yes	Fee
Mayer-Salovey-Caruso Emotional Intelligence Test (MSCEIT)	Emotional Intelligence	Yes	Fee
Keirsey Temperament Sorter	Personality	No	None
Myers Briggs Type Indicator	Psychological Type	Yes	Fee
Interest and Career			
Campbell Interest and Skill Survey	Interest, Skills, and Career	No	Fee
CareerKey	Interest, Skills, and Career	No	Fee
Motivational Assessment of Personal Potential (MAPP)	Interest and Career	No	Fee
Princeton Review Career Quiz	Interest and Career	No	None
Self-Directed Search Holland Interest Inventory	Interest and Career	No	Fee
Strong Interest Inventory	Interest and Career	No	Fee
Skill			
Career Assessment Exercises	Skill	No	None
Skills Center	Skill	No	None
What Is Your Skill Set?	Skill	No	None
Values			
Soul Survival: Career Values	Values	No	None
Value Questionnaire	Values	No	None

Source: Table adapted from the Riley Guide: Self-Assessment Resources June 2009

PERFORMANCE-BASED ASSESSMENTS

Other assessments may be available to you through your educational institution or, once you have secured a job, through your employer. Some of these include 360-degree assessments, annual performance reviews, competency models and assessments, or peer feedback within work projects or tasks. Each of these assessments represents an extremely valuable opportunity for learning and reflection, and to ignite change within yourself. Cynthia Egan, President of Retirement Plan Services at T. Rowe Price, commented on self-evaluation, sharing, "You can't skirt around your areas that need attention for development. Life is about trial and error and learning from these errors. Even with the most impactful career successes I've had, I still look at those experiences and think, 'What could have been done better?'" Similarly, Lora J. Villarreal, Ph.D., Executive Vice President and Chief People Officer at Affiliated Computer Services, Inc. (ACS), notes, "Every night I go home and ask myself, 'Was this an "A" day for me?'" No matter how senior one becomes in her career, self-reflection should not diminish or become less important. If anything, aspiring leaders require a healthy measure of self-exploration in order to stay current on their most compelling qualities and disadvantages.

WHAT IS YOUR PURPOSE?

Many times we impose limits on ourselves professionally without giving ourselves a chance to dream of what we really want. Purpose can emanate from your personal, professional, emotional, or spiritual side—or exist in combination. If you can understand and identify your sense of purpose, finding the right job will be much easier work. Cuc T. Vu, Chief Diversity Officer at Human Rights Campaign, was particularly passionate about this point when I interviewed her. She recommended, "Clarify your purpose and let everything else emanate from that. . . . Walk through the world as your complete self . . . find out what moves you!"

Sometimes a thought-provoking question is all it takes to help you dispel ambiguity and see things clearly. Consider the following questions as a way to answer the question, "What is your purpose?"

- If you had unlimited power, how would you use it?
- What did you love doing as a child?
- What do you love to do in your free time?
- When do people ask you for help?
- What is the *single* biggest barrier preventing you from leading?

- How would your professional biography read if you had the perfect career?
- When you get compliments at work, which ones are the most satisfying to hear?
- If money were not an issue, what kind of job would you pursue?
- What skills have always come easily to you?
- Is there a job you love so much that you would do it for free?
- Think about a time when you were happiest and most effective in a job. What were you doing?
- If you were on the cover of *Time* magazine, what would the cover caption say?
- What work activities have you engaged in where time seems to fly?
- Is your career a runaway success? If not, why?

DEVELOP YOUR DREAM BIO

Following is a revealing exercise I would like you to try: Consider what your dream biography would say. Take the time to consider, if there were no limits, what you would love to do professionally. Use your imagination and take your "whole" self into account as you jot down ideas. Try to keep your biography concise and to a maximum of three sentences. For example, I used writing my dream biography as a way to clarify what I really wanted. Here's what I wrote a few years ago:

> Selena Rezvani is a leading authority on Gen X and Y women and leadership. Leveraging her background in management consulting, she is in her "sweet spot" when coaching high-potential women aspiring to move into leadership. Selena has worked with numerous *Fortune* 100, government, and non-profit organizations to increase their representation of women leaders and has written many acclaimed publications geared at working women. She is also active in her favorite nonprofit, the National Association of Women MBAs, where she serves as a Regional Vice President.

While I have taken some deviations from this manifesto, I now live a life where I can say my actual biography looks more like this description than unlike it. What does your dream biography imply about you? As you craft your own biography, I recommend considering the following elements in your description:

- Your area of expertise
- Your passion or interest

- Your level of experience
- Your credibility, based on the types of companies that you have worked for
- Your credentials, for instance degrees, certifications, or publications
- Other significant roles you have held, such as nonprofit involvement
- Other aspirational tidbits, for example being the youngest vice president at a company or the valedictorian of your graduating class (Go with what excites you!)

You might also ask yourself where your biography would appear. Is it posted on your company's Web site? Is it featured in a conference brochure where you will be delivering a keynote address? Is it at the end of an article about you in *The Wall Street Journal?* Again, think BIG and let yourself go deeply into your visioning process!

JOURNALING

Increasingly, journaling is a core component of leadership classes and related training programs. Why? Journaling is an effective technique for reflecting on one's strengths or areas of weakness, or in response to a significant incident that shaped you in some way. Erin McGinnis, National Committee Chair of the Society of Women Engineers, suggests, "I think reflecting on your strengths and weaknesses is pretty important. . . . My boss blocks out 30 minutes a day to write in his journal so that he can record his experiences, reflect on them, and pass them down to his kids one day. So many of these business journals help you professionally and many best-selling business authors kept journals and later turned them into books."

Journaling is a process of self-development that aids progress and is helpful when used alone, in a group setting, or with a trusted advisor. Many women I interviewed suggested keeping logs or diaries of career successes and lessons learned to reflect upon. The concept of a professional diary fosters accountability and progress, and represents an organizational system for documenting your talents. Alexandra Miller, Chief Executive Officer of Mercedes Medical, Inc., encourages young women to use concrete strategies that encourage goal setting. She advised, "Focus like a laser beam on what you want. Set goals, and timelines on how you'll achieve them."

Documentation has a practical use as well; it becomes handy in hiring, promotion, and compensation conversations. Whereas many of us are used to engaging in verbal dialogue about our careers, journaling converts it to a tangible medium, thereby increasing our chances of accountability and effectiveness in meeting goals. Your journal can also be a reference that you consult to help substantiate how you have improved in an area.

Journals can be used in many forms; below I have listed some of the methods with which creative journaling can be most useful.

- Reflect on an area you are struggling with.
- Reflect on an area where you are thriving.
- Take time to daydream about your loftiest aspirations, documenting what the dream looks like. Consider how realizing your aspiration could change your life.
- Reflect on a single event or situation from a 360-degree perspective, taking into account multiple people's perceptions.
- Create a goal workbook with specific time limits for reaching your goals.
- Develop positive scenarios. Ask yourself questions that start with, "What if . . . ?"
- Write about the first business idea that comes to you and give yourself time and space to brainstorm in your journal.
- Consider engaging a journaling partner where you can have a dialogue and build upon each others' ideas.
- Keep a collection of pictures, quotes or symbols that inspire you. If you are so inclined, write about your reactions to these.
- Develop a list of pros and cons regarding any situation.
- Create a table where you write key ideas or events in one column and your personal reactions to them in another column. (The Double Entry method has long been used in education to help students separate fact from emotion.)
- Consider journaling as a means for creating a knowledge base or memory bank. As you continue to accumulate knowledge, you can organize, file, and sort your knowledge inventory, a job that is easier when your journal is electronic.

You can also ask yourself simple but provocative questions that stimulate your journaling experience. Below are some examples taken from *Journal Writing for Teachers and Students*. These questions can be used following any experience:

- **Descriptive**—What happened?
- **Metacognitive**—What were your thoughts, feelings, assumptions, beliefs, values, attitudes?
- **Analytic**—What were the reasoning and thinking behind actions and practices?
- **Evaluative**—What was good or bad? What are the implications?
- **Reconstructive**—What changes might be made? What are plans for future actions? (Mitchell and Coltrinari, 2001)

GETTING A COACH

Another way to tap into your passion is to engage a coach. Coaching is the practice of meeting with a credentialed, trained, or experienced professional who helps individuals identify their career interests, secure a new job, and strategize about career management and promotions. Career coaches can even help people transition back into the workforce after children or other significant life changes. How do you use a coach? As the recipient of these services, you can and should ask career coaches for an explanation of their services, fees, and ethical guidelines before getting involved. Professional career counselors are expected to follow the ethical guidelines of organizations such as the National Career Development Association, the National Board for Certified Counselors, the American Counseling Association, or the American Psychological Association. Professional codes of ethics discourage unreasonable fees, violations of confidentiality, and unrealistic guarantees made to clients.

The benefits of engaging a career coach are many. For one, you have a sounding board in a career coach with whom you can process your career history and brainstorm ideas for the future. Career coaches, because of their experience and training, are full of strategies and exercises to help people move out of stagnation and into action. The best career coach provides an outside, objective perspective and has good insight into what recruiters and human resources companies want.

A good matchmaker of people's skills and jobs, a career coach should help you determine your needs, maximize your strengths, and help you gain momentum in your job search and self-exploration. Jeanine Becker has used coaches and found that it paved the way to her ideal blended career. She recalled, "I've written in a journal and worked with various coaches to gain a clear vision of what I'm looking for in my career, what was missing, what excites me, where I excel, and what the key values are that drive me. That awareness has informed each step I've taken and this is ultimately what moved me to pursue teaching, training, and coaching."

A skilled career coach will help you gain new skills for managing your career and avoid repeating past mistakes you have made. According to Dr. Randall Hansen, career expert and coach, coaching should provide you with clear, tangible outcomes, including:

1. Enhanced self-awareness and direction
2. Clarity of career and job-search goals
3. Increased career management skills
4. Overall improvement of your quality of life

The Career Coach Institute offers resources on coaching and provides a directory of career coaches from which to choose. The National Career Development Association (NCDA) is a founding division of the American Counseling Association, and promotes the career development of all people over the life span. NCDA offers a directory, which allows you to search for Master Career Counselors (MCC) and Master Career Development Professionals (MCDP).

TEST-DRIVING JOBS AND INDUSTRIES

Many people have found their ideal career through a series of trial and error. Jeanine Becker reflected, "I've learned that . . . insight may not come while sitting on your couch pondering what's next. . . . See what you enjoy—not just the title and job description, but what the work is actually like on a day-to-day basis. You'll know what feels right, what you excel at—when you do it."

I encourage young women to experiment with different jobs and industries. Firsthand experience is always the best indicator of job fit; no book, movie, or secondhand account will rightly convey what *you* will feel like in a given profession. I should note, however, that some employers may hold it against you if, for example, they see that your résumé contains several sequential, totally unrelated jobs. Keep in mind that as you test out different roles and companies, you will need to be prepared with some kind of rationale for the roles you took. Recruiters and HR departments tend to prefer people with career paths that seem thought-out, compared to a profile where a person randomly "landed" in each job without forethought. I encourage you to try things and get invaluable firsthand work experience. But, unless you are making a 180-degree career change, be ready to weave a common thread throughout your jobs that can help explain the career decisions you have made.

A FOOT IN THE DOOR

Before you can get an "in" with an organization where you would like to work, it can help to identify a list of potential employers. This list may come from job searches you do, word-of-mouth recommendations from your network, college career centers, or your own research. First, consider if you have contacts at any of the companies you are interested in. Managing your contacts can be made easier with professional networking sites such as LinkedIn.com and Doostang.com, which allow you to keep all your contacts in one place. I particularly like LinkedIn as you can also join online groups and easily engage in discussions. You might also use these sites to identify individuals who have your dream job, or HR contacts at key companies. Once you secure a short list of companies and contacts, do not be shy about reaching out to people. You can write to individuals to ask if they would be willing to talk to you about how they secured their current job, what experiences served them well, and what educational background was required, if any. Use your existing academic, personal, and professional networks to communicate what type of job or company you are looking to find, and feel free to ask if others can help introduce you to key people.

I also recommend that women approach companies they are interested in working for with the request for an informational interview. An informational interview gives the company a chance to tell someone new about what they do, market their products and services, and meet new talent. An interviewee can also benefit from such a meeting by forming a relationship with a company and one of its representatives, thereby getting closer to a job interview than the average faceless, nameless online job applicant. It is important to be prepared for an informational interview by preparing questions and knowing ahead of time where you could best fit into the organization. By requesting an informational interview, you will become an *actual* person in the eyes of the recruiter, and can be seen as ambitious, self-motivated, and action-oriented. If the interview goes well and you have interest in the company, make that fact known and keep in touch with the recruiter regarding open positions. Just as you should in a job interview, be sure to send a written thank you letter to the person who interviewed you and reiterate why you believe you would be an asset to the company. You might maintain the relationship by checking on job availability occasionally or sending a relevant news story or article to your contact. Doing so will maintain the relationship and keep you at the top of the employer's mind.

JOB INTERVIEWING 101

As you maneuver to get your foot in the door, you will likely be going on in-person job interviews or partaking in telephone interviews. To be clear, your goal as an interviewee is twofold; you need to gather enough information to decide if you want to work at a company, and you need to convince the interviewer that you are *the* candidate for the position. Remember, the interviewer's primary purpose is to promote the company while attracting and hiring the best possible candidate for the job. If you have completed some self-assessments and considered what your most closely held values are, interviewing will be significantly easier for you. If not, at a minimum, you should consider the following questions as a way to prepare for an interview. Chances are good that you will be asked some variant of the following questions:

- Why do you want to work here?
- What are your areas of strength?
- What do you need to improve upon?
- What distinguishes you from other candidates? What is special and unique about you?
- How are your past skills and experiences transferable to this position and this company?
- How do you envision the next five to ten years of your career?
- When have you been most challenged in your career? How did you manage it?
- What are your most significant professional successes?
- What is your management style (regarding projects and people)?
- How well do you collaborate with others?
- How well do you work independently?

EMPLOYER RESEARCH

As you prepare for an interview, make sure to research the organization beforehand. Visiting the company's Web site represents a natural starting place. You might also consider downloading the company's brochure, annual report, or 10-K for perusal. Publicly traded companies are required to file 10-K reports annually with the Securities and Exchange Commission (SEC). 10-Ks are similar to a company's annual report, but highlight more details about its management, financial situation, and practices. 10-Ks also include the bylaws of a company and pertinent legal information. In addition, many women have found it helpful to research whether or not the company is considered a top employer, by outlets such as *Working Mother* Magazine, *Fortune*'s 100 Best Places to Work in America, DiversityInc's Top 50 Companies for Diversity, or any of the other regional and local employer rankings that are available. I recommend that you also do research to understand how representative women are in the leadership of the company. Catherine J. Mathis commented on this fact, recalling, "When interviewing at the *New York Times*, I was struck by the fact that three quarters of the people I met with were women. Moreover, these women were high ranking—a VP, an SVP, and a CFO. Having come from the very male-dominated shipping industry, I was very impressed."

As you prepare to be interviewed, be sure that you can answer basic questions about the firm before meeting with any of its representatives, such as:

- What does the company do?
- What are the company's mission, vision, and values?

- When was the company started?
- What do the company's financial or other performance indicators show?
- Who is the main consumer base of the company's products/services?
- What does the competitive landscape look like for this company?
- Where are the company's locations?
- How many employees work at the company?
- What kind of public image/brand does the company have?
- Is there important terminology the company uses (i.e., do they call employees "associates"?)?

GETTING THE INTERVIEW RIGHT

You should be prepared to engage in interviews in different formats, ranging from telephone conversations, to formal dinners, to casual coffee shops, and, of course, in traditional office environments. If you are ever faced with a choice as to whether to meet in person or via telephone, always opt for the in-person option. Meeting in-person tends to showcase more of your skills and personality, and allows you to be more agile in the interview, reacting to body language and other in-person clues you can collect "in the moment." If you are less-than-experienced at interviewing, I recommend doing at least one role-play of the interview with a trusted friend, professor, or mentor. Role-playing can help you curb your interview nerves because it makes the real interview feel more predictable, as though you have already been there.

Since you have done your homework by this point, be confident in an interview and when answering questions, focus on keeping your responses clear, articulate, and evidence-based. What specific scenarios can you share that highlight your skills? Too many interviewees speak in general terms, so the more you can give examples and show measurable change or progress, the better. Think about times you have truly shone, or when you were offered praise for your work. Was there a project you worked on where you had great synergy with your team or the task at hand? Are there compelling metrics that illustrate how you added value to the company?

If you have learned that the company uses certain terminology, such as favoring "business unit" to "department," or "associate" to "employee," do your best to use that same language. It will help send the message that you can easily integrate into their culture and fit in. No matter where you are in your career, even if you are still in college, you should be prepared to think through the tough interview questions you may be asked and have answers ready. People may ask why your grade point average is low, why you have never stayed at a job for longer than two years, or why your college major is so different from the job you want. Think through what your vulnerabilities are as a candidate. Again, use role-playing to prepare for the hard questions. Requesting that your friend or mentor ask you some tough questions will help you feel more in control during the "real thing."

ASKING *THEM* QUESTIONS

An easy rule of thumb to remember is that you should always ask questions in an interview . . . and I mean always. If you know that you will be meeting with many people over the course of an interview visit, prepare several different questions to ask. Asking questions shows you are hungry to learn about the company and role and shows humility that you do not yet have the company "all figured out." Most of all, asking good questions guards against the worst kind of interview position—apathy. Appearing apathetic is the worst crime that an interviewee can perpetrate! Even if you do not like a company or job based on an interview, treat the interview as though you want the job. Put forward your most professional self and then think through the job fit off the interview clock.

Ideally, your questions should reflect a mix of subjects. Some questions can address tangibles such as benefits and promotion policies, while others can be specific to the work or based on something you heard in the job interview itself.

QUESTIONS TO ASK IN AN INTERVIEW

- What are the two most critical skills needed for this position?
- Where does this position fit within the organization?
- If the ideal candidate were hired in this role, what kind of change would it create in the organization?
- How would you describe the corporate culture?
- What is your vision for this position?
- What else can I tell you about my qualifications?
- What kind of assignments will the incumbent work on?
- Is there an emphasis on creating career paths for employees? If so, how?
- How do you measure performance?
- Do you see this job as more team-focused or independent in nature?
- What background would the perfect candidate for this job have?
- Is it common practice here to promote from within?
- What challenges does the company face?
- How would you describe the management style here?

- What characteristics do top performers at this company have in common?
- What distinguishes you most from your competitors?
- What new customer base would you like to target?
- Do you offer training or tuition assistance to employees?
- How affected is your company by shifts in your larger industry? Can you give me an example?
- What are some of the strengths and weaknesses of the organization?
- What is it like to work here?
- What have you enjoyed most about your time with the organization?
- Where is your organization looking to grow and develop?
- How do departments work together here? Does this position have exposure to other departments?
- What kind of timeline are you working with to fill this position?
- What are the next steps in your process?

Ultimately, the message you want to send if you are interested in an opportunity, is just that—interest. You want to avoid conveying desperation, extreme nervousness, indifference, or apathy. If you are interested in the job, go ahead and show your genuine enthusiasm. In my experience, I have observed that most employers would rather hire someone moderately qualified who really wants the job, in favor of a highly qualified person who seems aloof or indifferent.

YOUR DREAM CAREER IS AROUND THE CORNER

Preparing for your dream job requires a multifaceted approach and different forms of exploration. While some of the preparation involves practical tasks such as researching and properly positioning yourself, other aspects require looking "within" to reflect on your deepest passions, interests, skills, and values. As D'Arcy Foster Rudnay, Senior Vice President for Comcast Corporation, points out, "Self-reflection is something you have to keep doing and that will help you navigate your entire career. Reflecting on your strengths and weaknesses helps you know what your best skills are, and what you are most respected for." In addition, finding passion in your work can reduce your stress level, increase your sense of well-being, and build your confidence. More than just a "nice-to-have," passion has the effect of making us more persistent and tenacious in our careers, and subsequently more successful. Taking the time to position yourself for a career with meaning is a worthy investment of your time; it will reflect on you positively as an employee and simultaneously feed you personally.

3

SUCCEEDING ON THE JOB

ON-THE-JOB RULES

As you transition from interviewee to job incumbent, there are a set of important strategies that can help you thrive on the job. Navigating the work world requires learning many written and unwritten rules—most of which were not originated by women. While some of these rules are specific to your company's culture and inner workings, many strategies for succeeding are quite universal across different companies. Presented in this chapter are the nuggets gleaned from the interviews I conducted with executives, including revelations many wished they had learned on the job sooner, or those lessons they learned the hard way.

YOUR JOB MIX

As you consider the makeup of your own position, you will realize that jobs require a mix of "technical" competencies as well as "general" competencies. Technical competencies are those areas that are unique to your job, industry, or function, in which you have special training or experience. Graphic design abilities, accounting acumen, and selling skills are all examples of technical competencies. General competencies, however, help you to be successful in most any job and are universally required in the workplace. Examples include written or oral communication, teamwork, or a "results" orientation. Every job requires a combination of general *and* technical skills, and the sooner you can identify the ones that are central to your role, the better off you will be.

GETTING THE FOUNDATION RIGHT

I strongly encourage those new to a position to master the foundational, critical skills of the job before focusing on any other activities. Particularly for those that are new to a job, it can take at least six months to grasp what is expected of you in your role, and closer to a year to learn how to perform all the necessary aspects of it. During this initial period, you will need to put most of your energy into learning the stated job duties expected of you as well as those that are more implicit. By focusing on these core activities and mastering them early on, you can begin to convey your credibility to your organization—an extremely important task for an aspiring leader. The command of your core duties is similar to the solid foundation of a building. Added activities like networking and attendance at conferences can serve to reinforce the building, but not if the foundation they sit on is cracked or shaky. Rather than distracting yourself with a barrage of internal and external activities early on, be persistent in learning your main job duties and becoming knowledgeable and proficient in them. You can engage in countless activities later in your tenure that will build upon and leverage these core competencies.

While competency at your basic job functions is critical, I do not necessarily believe that a woman needs to have an "A+" command of her field in order for her career to be a runaway success. Why? Many women I have interviewed reflected that they succeeded not because they were the best technical experts at their particular job. These women had *enough* knowledge to perform their core job duties competently, but the key differentiator was that they leveraged other strong skills to achieve great success. According to DeeDee Wilson, Chief Financial Officer at Aritzia, "Too often, women are focused on technical training, believing that if we are really good at our jobs, we will ultimately be rewarded. I think finding your voice as a leader is perhaps more important than getting more proficient in your technical role as you are moving higher in an organization."

Consider which of these examples represents a more successful business leader. Person A has a just-above-average level of technical competence but the ability to inspire and motivate the employees of the organization. Person B is a known technical expert in her field but prefers solitude and working with data to working with people. No contest between the two, right? Clearly, both of these examples highlight individuals who can attain success. However, I challenge the notion that the best leaders must always be the most proficient technically. I suggest leveraging and maximizing your combined skills; both those that are natural and those you have developed over time. Dale Carnegie, the famous American writer and lecturer on self-development, supported this thinking saying, "Even in such technical lines as engineering, about 15% of one's . . . success is due [to] one's technical knowledge and about 85% is due to skill in human engineering, to personality and the ability to lead people" (Carnegie, 1982). The best leaders do not just have a command of where they excel, they also know their weaknesses. They surround themselves with smart people that can fill their knowledge gaps. Each of us needs to possess a combination of role-based and interpersonal qualities to succeed as leaders, as technical prowess alone will never be a guaranteed pathway to advancement.

Take Jill for example. Jill is an accountant—a role where she is expected, at a minimum, to have a "basic" ability to prepare balance sheets, profit-and-loss statements, and other financial reports. Jill has an average level of comfort with financial data that allows her to accurately analyze trends, costs, and revenues, and to predict future revenues and expenses. Jill believes she is an all-around good employee, but she is seen by her organization and boss as being exceptional. The key to Jill's successful reputation is that she leverages her greatest and most natural strengths to augment her technical performance. In reality, Jill may have an average level of competence at accounting, but she happens to be a skilled "people person." She can put people at ease, resolve disputes, and bring the best out in a group. Contributing these skills to her organization has helped grow her professional reputation exponentially. She has built bridges across the company and helped the accounting department be seen as an important group that is collaborative, visible, and cooperative. Prior to her tenure, the accounting department was largely seen as hard to work with and an obstacle people needed to "work around."

START WITH THE END IN MIND

Even if you are not *the* star technical performer at your organization, what other skills can you leverage and utilize? Where could you add more value to your organization? Which of your best skills go largely untapped? Remember, your total contribution to your organization is made up of far more than just your specialized knowledge.

Once you have considered your answers to these questions, take the time to ask yourself how you would like to be remembered. Answer the question, "What would I like my legacy to be at this company?" Crafting an answer to this question can serve as a guiding mission statement for the rest of your time with the organization. It also gives you a personal vision to strive toward and uphold. One example of a legacy statement is, "I'd like to be remembered for making this place better than when I started. I will be seen as someone who mentored and developed others, treated my fellow employees as though they were my best customers, and took this department from fragmented and reactive, to a smooth-running operation." Will your legacy be comprised of improvements you made, uncharted job tasks you performed, people you built relationships with, or the way you handled adversity? Reflecting on how you want to be remembered will help sharpen your focus and keep you on track toward your goals.

Once you have built an unshakable foundation at your job, consider how you can maximize your combined skill set by continuing to build your contribution. Below are some examples and activities that can propel your job further, cementing your positive reputation. They are categorized into areas where you can use your interpersonal skills or technical skills. Taking on such additional activities, once you are competent in your role, can help to brand you as proactive and solution-oriented. Beyond enhancing your résumé, participating in the activities shown in Table 3.1 can also expose you to senior management and departments other than your own.

GENERALIST OR SPECIALIST?

When contemplating the direction of your career, you may want to consider if you will be better served by becoming a specialist in a certain field or more of a generalist. While a generalist is an all-rounder who knows "enough" about many subjects, a specialist hones her skills so that she has

Table 3.1   Skills and On-the-Job Activities

Skills	On-the-Job Activities
Interpersonal skills	Create alliances in the organization not in place currently
	Start an affinity group, special interest group, or taskforce to resolve a problem or make an improvement
	Cultivate relationships or alliances with other well-matched partner organizations
	Volunteer to promote your organization at trade shows or other events
	Use creative channels and interpersonal acumen to generate new business
Technical skills	Offer a lunchtime brown-bag education session in an area where you are knowledgeable and others want to learn
	Participate in an industry panel at a university, company, or association
	Write an article for publication in your area of strength
	Do industry benchmarking or market research to see how your company fares compared to others
	Give a talk at a networking event or conference in your area of technical strength

deep knowledge in one area. Consider how you want to either broaden or focus your skills to inform your future career. Professionals can be successful whether they choose a generalist or a specialist path; however, the women in leadership I interviewed almost always pointed out that they had a number of broad experiences, which helped them lead more effectively. Carla E. Lucchino, Assistant Deputy Commandant, Installations and Logistics at the U.S. Marine Corps, advised, "People should not just become expert in one thing. They should get broad, well-rounded knowledge. It really helped me to move around a lot—both geographically and from job to job. In the Department of Defense, they grow generals by exposing them to many different areas. I mimicked that style and it's helped me quite a bit."

More women than not pointed out that their broad range of skills gave them invaluable exposure, positioning them well when it came to leading. Experimenting with different roles and seeking new challenges also helped stretch many women I interviewed outside of their comfort zones. In fact several interviewees shared that they became so comfortable with challenge that it no longer rattled them in a profound way. Illustrating this point, Autumn Bayles, Senior Vice President of Strategic Operations at Tasty Baking Company recounted, "One of my former supervisors said to me, 'Autumn, don't just always do what you're good at.' I've used that as a mantra and become a jack of all trades."

Since the view "at the top" requires a working knowledge of many business units and functions, it is the ability to understand the interrelationship between business units that matters most, not necessarily a deep understanding of one of them in particular. Alexandra Miller, Chief Executive Officer of Mercedes Medical, Inc., asserted, "What has allowed me to be most successful at work is focus, drive, and an ability to see the 'big picture.'" In Alexandra's case, she learned to see the big picture by working in sales, marketing, purchasing, and accounting functions before becoming a chief operating officer, and later a chief executive officer. Consider how you can get broader exposure to different functions, even if you do not choose to do something as dramatic as change job functions. Many avenues exist to help with this, from participating in cross-functional taskforces at work, to partaking in a rotational program with your company, or asking your boss for opportunities to serve on projects that involve multiple divisions.

Barbara A. F. Greene, Chief Executive Officer of Greene and Associates, Inc., built on this idea in her interview, encouraging, "Think big! Regardless of your role in a company, you have to connect it to the big picture. You must think enterprise-wide. The further you move up, the more you will hear the terms 'strategic' and 'visionary.' Too many people think that if they're an expert in one area, they don't need to know about other areas. This is not true."

Yet another positive aspect of a generalist approach is that it helps you get comfortable explaining different concepts to different audiences. Cynthia Egan, President of Retirement Plan Services at T. Rowe Price, credited "being able to communicate complex thoughts in a clear, succinct way" as a skill that has made her "promotable." Many women I interviewed advised that young women should become proficient at explaining complicated ideas in an understandable way. It only makes sense that exposure to different functions would help a woman to understand terminology and speak a common language that she can articulately convey to others.

BECOMING INDISPENSABLE

In this day of outsourced jobs and automation, it is important to find ways to become indispensable to your organization, your division—and your boss. An indispensable employee has an expertise that is critical to their organization, and often not easy to come by. Being indispensable creates a reliance on you as an employee that can translate to having more choice in work assignments, better job opportunities, and added bargaining chips when it comes to salary negotiation. Consider what you do (or could do) that is *absolutely critical* to your organization. Remember that critical skills can be as concrete as being an expert at a hard-to-use technological tool, or as intangible as getting two divisions to work more collaboratively together. Below are some questions to ask yourself in leveraging your strengths and contributions to your organization:

- What is unique or special about what I bring to my organization?
- What technical capabilities do I perform best?
- When do coworkers compliment me? What skills am I using when I receive compliments?
- What do I do that no one can do better?
- In which areas do I receive my best feedback in performance reviews?
- In what areas do I take on more than I am expected to accomplish?
- Do others depend on me for certain knowledge or skills? To what extent?
- What about my contributions are hard to replace?
- What kinds of skills does my organization need more of now? In the future?
- Do I train or mentor others to do work that is indispensable?
- How do I connect my individual work to my department's goals, and to my organization's objectives?
- In which areas do people say I am "a natural"?
- What are my most important interpersonal qualities?

Remember that your ability to develop unique expertise will make you more valuable to your organization, better protected from a job security perspective, and more attractive to other employers. Locate what is unique about your contributions, and build on your uniqueness. Take initiative by spearheading an organizational improvement effort, or going the extra mile to find a new angle to solve a problem. If you believe there is an overlooked or important opportunity for your division or company, take the reins by writing a business case in support of a change or compiling confirmatory research. Katharine Weymouth, Publisher of the *Washington Post* and Chief Executive Officer of Washington Post Media, reinforces the importance of taking initiative, advising, "Continuously go above and beyond in your work. Don't send the message that you're too good for a job, do the bare minimum or just 'punch the clock.'" By harnessing relationships, building cooperation, and filling organizational gaps, you will gain tremendous learning. You will also benefit professionally in short- and long-term ways. People who have the combination of needed skills and a proactive approach will always stand out in a crowd. Furthermore, members of this group are better positioned for job security and career advancement.

Cynthia Egan continually asks herself one powerful question to assess her contribution. She asks, "What does it mean to create value for the organization—and does everything we do support this?" As you build your intellectual and experiential capital at a company, you should always be asking yourself how you create value for your organization. Keep in mind that the value you create can and should take several forms. Remember though—none of your unique contributions matter very much if management is not aware of them. Make your senior and imme-diate management aware of your unique abilities by communicating the level at which you are depended on to perform the duties. Are you relied on weekly or daily to provide a service? If so, communicate that reality to higher-ups and try to accurately forecast if people's dependence on you will increase.

YOUR PRESENCE

When it comes to work, it matters how you present yourself at every turn. Developing your presence is also critical as a leader. So what is pres-ence and why does it matter? Presence is about carrying yourself in such a way that you are seen as credible and truly heard. Women with presence are able to motivate and persuade others, are respected, and have a certain command that inspires the "followership" of the people around them. Your presence can be positional, as represented by your job role, title, or place in the organizational hierarchy, or it can be interpersonal.

Jo Miller, Chief Executive Officer of Women's Leadership Coaching Inc., has coached many professional women and has found that both positional and interpersonal presence are often underleveraged by women. In Jo's experience, women can de-emphasize their stature by providing oversimplified introductions like, "Hi, I'm Andy from Operations." Jo taught me a simple but wonderful exercise to counteract this habit. Jo encourages women to come up with a "30-second commercial" that harnesses their full importance and position. In order to develop your own commercial, fill in answers to the four items below, synthesizing them into a short paragraph.

1. Hi, my name is . . . [Add Name]
2. I am a . . . [Add Title]
3. I . . . [Add key job duties]
4. Please come directly to me if . . . [Add ways you can be of service to others]

Some examples of effective commercials are:

- "Hi, my name is Lydia Mendoza. I am a senior communications manager. I work in the marketing division where I create, implement, and oversee communications programs that promote our organization. Specifically, I develop materials like graphics, brochures, fact sheets, logos, and other promotional products. Please come to me directly if you have a need for marketing materials or any questions about developing or distributing them."
- "Hi, my name is Nina Singh. I am an admissions representative here at the university. I am responsible for recruiting prospective students and providing guidance throughout the admissions process. I lead group information sessions and coordinate campus tours for students and parents. I also provide training to all schools of the university on our admissions processes. Please come to me directly if you have any questions about admissions."
- "I'm Samantha Reynolds, call center quality analyst. I screen incoming and outgoing calls to ensure quality, customer service, and adherence to our company's policies and procedures. I provide feedback to call center representatives and develop analyses based on performance goals. The best part of my job is developing and delivering training programs to call center staff. Please come to me directly if you have any call center issue or need."

Consider how you introduce yourself to people currently. Is your message crisp, concise, and compelling? Do you say it confidently? Refine your commercial, keeping it to 30 seconds, by following Jo's steps above rather than leaving introductions to chance. Be sure to write down your commercial so that you can refer to it in the future. Keep in mind that you will want to tailor your commercial depending on your audience. If you are interacting with a group of technical people in your field, you may want to give more details on your expertise than you would to a group of mixed departments at your company. This exercise can be done by anyone, in any role or job, which is why it is such a useful tool. Your commercial will change over time as you adopt new duties, so keep thinking of ways to refresh your message.

BODY LANGUAGE AND PRESENCE

Body language can send many messages about you, often times without you realizing it. Body language is so important in conveying your presence, in fact, that some research shows it is more important than what you actually say. Albert Mehrabian, Professor Emeritus of Psychology at UCLA, found through his research that there are three elements that influence an audience most when a communicator is talking about their feelings or attitudes. Through his experiments, Mehrabian ranked the top three elements in order of importance to audiences, which has become known widely as the "7%–38%–55% Rule." This rule shows that an audience's perception of you is made up of your verbal ability (7%), your vocal ability (35%), and your visual presence (55%) (Mehrabian, 1971).

From this research, we can deduce that nonverbal elements of communication help listeners to fully grasp a communicator's message, thoughts, and feelings. Furthermore, body language can serve to support your verbal communication or contradict it. Interestingly, Mehrabian found that if words and body language disagree, the audience tends to believe what the body language is communicating in favor of the words they are hearing. A critical strategy, therefore, is to try to make sure that you are aware of your words, tone, and body language, including how they correspond to each other.

HOW YOU LOOK AT WORK

Your physical appearance is another aspect of your presence that can help to build or undermine your credibility more than you realize. The more you look the part of a professional, the more other people will see you as someone who should be taken seriously. Conversely, the more you present yourself as unpolished or messy, the more it sends the message that *you* are unpolished or a mess. Carla E. Lucchino noted, "The way a woman behaves and dresses for example are important in terms of how they're seen. I've seen many women either dress like a little girl or dress too provocatively and inadvertently get the wrong kind of reaction for it." Why distract people from the positive contributions you can make by looking unprofessional? Whether or not it is fair to be judged on appearance, the reality is that our culture operates with a heavy focus on physicality. Employers are looking for people who will make good representatives of their companies inside and outside of company walls, and it behooves employers to find people who look the part of the professional.

Members of Generation Y, in particular, have garnered a reputation for workplace informality—particularly when it comes to appearance. Despite this trend, many workplaces are not relaxing their dress standards to the same extent as their youngest employees. Donna Callejon, Chief Operating Officer at GlobalGiving, advised, "Even though our society is getting more informal and casual, always dress professionally." Donna's urging to consistently dress professionally is simple advice and yet often overlooked. I have never observed the habit of "dressing down" at work help anyone professionally. However, I have seen example after example of people who negotiated a promotion by embodying the inner and outer characteristics of leaders at their organization. Quite simply, by looking and acting the part of a leader, you are making it harder for your employer to refuse your career advancement.

A commonly heard workplace saying is, "Dress for the job you want, not the job you have." I could not agree more with this sentiment. Successful career advancement requires planning and a forward-thinking strategy. Dressing "the part" sends the message that you are ready *now* for whatever role you are personifying. Courteney Monroe, Executive Vice President of Consumer Marketing at HBO, recalls, "My grandfather told me to dress the way my superiors dress. Many times I resisted dressing 'down' and I think it's benefited me." Dressing a step above your current position is a simple and relatively easy career strategy to implement. It is not one that you need to over-think; just look at those above you for guidance. Consider these simple guidelines:

- Identify successful women in your organization who are at a level where you would like to be. Observe how they carry themselves and what they wear to work.
- Dress in a way that reflects the job you want, not the job you have.
- When in doubt about whether to dress up or dress down, always dress up. At work-related events, it is always better to be overdressed than underdressed.

YOUR PHYSICALITY

Your height and physical stature, particularly if you are slight or small, can be a factor to consider when developing your presence. For many women, smaller size or stature can make them feel less noticed by others, but this does not need to be the case. Melissa M. Monk, Chief Infrastructure Officer at Capital One, recalled, "Since 1993, I've had an amazing mentor who I admire immensely. . . . She is an example of the fact that physical stature in no way equates to presence. While she is very petite, one never noticed. All you saw was her passion, commitment, strength, and influence." Melissa's example underscores that you can be remembered more for your contributions than for your physique. Consider the following strategies as guideposts:

- Project your voice: When you are speaking, project your voice at a level that sounds assertive and confident. Practice speaking confidently—no matter what you are saying—by projecting your voice and finding your "perfect" volume.
- Confident posture: Posture is conveyed from the way you sit to how you walk and carry yourself. When attending a meeting, sit upright with an open torso, which shows both comfort and confidence. If standing or presenting, keep your posture open with your torso facing your audience and maintain strong eye contact with the audience.
- Eye contact: Make strong eye contact with everyone from the receptionist to the chief executive of your company. Resist the urge to look down or look away if you are nervous. Being mindful about keeping strong eye contact can help build your confidence and send the message that you are interested, engaged, and self-assured.
- A firm handshake: A strong, firm handshake communicates to those you are meeting that you are someone to be taken seriously. A firm handshake is best executed while making full, friendly eye contact.

Rosslyn Kleeman, Chair of the Coalition for Effective Change, reinforced the importance of presentation, noting, "I think how you present yourself is crucial . . . [w]hether you're presenting on stage, one[-]on[-]one, or in an interview." To Rosslyn's point, the importance of presence should not be underestimated. Working on your presence will help you feel more comfortable in your skin and allow you to fully project your confidence. Confidence can lead to speaking your mind more often, venturing your ideas, and taking smart, educated risks. What kind of presence would you like to be remembered for? Is there someone at your company who has great presence and who you can emulate and mimic?

As you speak your ideas, remember to leave out the qualifiers that women are often accustomed to using when sharing their viewpoint. According to gender and communication expert Connie Glaser, these statements, which tend to cancel out what you say, can include, "This might be a stupid question . . . ," "I'm not really versed about this . . . ," or "You might already know this . . . ." Another common disqualifier noted by Glaser is to apologize too frequently (Glaser, 2007). Generation X and Y women are particularly vulnerable to using these disqualifiers since they have less experience and confidence than their older counterparts. Each time you are tempted to qualify what you will say, try leaving the qualifier out and just sharing your thought or idea. As you venture more opinions free of qualification, you will gain confidence!

A STRATEGIC VIEW OF THE ORGANIZATION

Do you tend to see things from the "detail" perspective or from more of a bird's eye viewpoint? The vast majority of leaders I interviewed credited thinking strategically, or "organization-wide," as a major asset in being promoted to leadership. Demonstrating that you do not just see your work from the perspective of your specific department, but rather from the perspective of the whole organization shows you are aware of the larger ramifications, both positive and negative, of your organization's actions. When I asked Melissa Monk what competencies made her "promotable," she offered, "Being able to think strategically with a broad view of the business." Similarly, DeeDee Wilson reflected, "As women, our nature is to be perfectionist and to spend too much time on the tasks rather than the big picture. The issue is that you can be seen as too much of a detail person and not enough of a strategic thinker. My mentor reminds me of this, which has really helped me."

On the same topic, Vicki Ho, General Manager, Asia Services for GE Healthcare Clinical Services at General Electric, reflected, "As you gain more credibility, you'll get more responsibility and must show that you can think strategically. For me, strategic thinking is about observation and contemplation. Consulting was great training for strategic thinking because you are always communicating with senior level people." Being a leader means seeing a broad view of the business. Get in the habit of seeing the big picture sooner rather than later and you will convey one of the most critical leadership competencies.

When you are mired in the details of your work, try asking yourself and your work group questions that cut through the myopic clutter. Some examples include:

- How will this initiative affect the larger business?
- Is this decision going to create a ripple effect in the organization?
- Is the impact of this decision to our collective benefit?

COMFORT WITH NUMBERS

My interviews, along with my own observations, point to a troubling finding relating to women and numbers. The perception exists that women are somehow less adept, less interested, or altogether allergic to finance or math and their applications to the job. What a truly useless perception! One of the many unfortunate things about such a sentiment is that it can hold a woman back from career opportunities that she feels otherwise equipped for, whether or not the perception of her math skill is actually correct. It can also create a psychological barrier in which a woman gets in her own way to success. Furthermore, such a stereotype does nothing to improve women's representation at the top of companies, or their potential to become high earners in scientific and math-oriented jobs.

Vicki Ho talked about the differences in how those in numbers-oriented versus other roles are perceived. She noted, "Many people see leadership roles for women as being in HR-type functions only. There is a perception that women are not tough enough for some of the more technical roles, but, fortunately, more women are moving into these areas. Once a woman is in a lead technical role—like in the area of finance—she is no longer questioned for being tough enough. People are more concerned about how smart and technically competent she is."

Catherine J. Mathis, Senior Vice President of Corporate Communications at The New York Times Company, advised, "I'm a huge proponent of women understanding finance, accounting and economics. I believe all business professionals need a strong foundation in these areas, especially finance; it can be one more arrow in their quiver. Some women seem to have some kind of phobia about finance despite the fact that it's a vital tool and the *lingua franca* of business." Similarly, Donna Callejon shared, "Many women tend to take jobs that require less of a 'bottom-line' orientation. I think it's important to have some analytical rigor within your skill base. I've been helped in every single job I've had by having training in economics."

In their eye-opening book *Failing at Fairness*, husband and wife team Myra and David Sadker discuss how our education system has historically failed girls. The Sadkers conducted numerous studies where they observed differences between how boys and girls were educated in the public school system. They explained in their research findings that there is "a syntax of sexism so elusive that most teachers and students were completely unaware of its influence" (Sadker & Sadker, 1995). The subtle, elusive nature of gender bias in schools shaped many people's paradigm of adolescent and adult females' capabilities. As men and women, we carry our early conditioning into the workplace as adults. As the messages that we deliver to our own children change and improve over time, expectantly the perception of a female math deficiency will diminish and eventually die.

Despite stereotypes of women and math, research substantiates that women are indeed equal to men in mathematical abilities. A recent study in *Science,* for example, showed that girls score just as well as boys in standardized math tests in the United States. Janet Hyde and her colleagues evaluated yearly math tests as required by the *No Child Left Behind* education law in 2002. Hyde's research team was able to compare the performance of over 7 million children—across 10 states—by gender. Their finding was that there was no difference in the scores of boys versus girls, not even in high school (Hyde at al., 2008). Whether or not negative perceptions of women and math stem from society at-large, our gender-specific conditioning, or other factors, messages that we heard as girls clearly affected how proficient we and others think we can be at math.

Summarizing how "numbers knowledge" has helped her career, Lora J. Villarreal, Ph.D., Executive Vice President and Chief People Officer at Affiliated Computer Services, Inc. (ACS), noted, "You need a working, functional knowledge of numbers—this has been very important for me. It doesn't matter what role you have, you will always need to prove your end performance by using numbers. You need to speak and understand the numbers language like everyone else." Leaders clearly require the ability to quantify activities in the workplace and women are undoubtedly capable of performing in this regard. In many types of jobs, figures need to be predicted futuristically, measured historically, or calculated based on certain conditions. If a job with a quantitative component presents itself, do not discount your skills or abilities based on outmoded, archaic stereotypes. Try it before you dismiss it!

A POSITIVE APPROACH CAN BE LEADERSHIP GOLD

Believe it or not, being positive at work can be a powerful tool for moving upward. As a starting point, people prefer the company of those that are positive to those that are negative. And people's preference, or view of your likeability, often plays a role in career advancement. Supporting this point, Maya Rockeymoore, Ph.D., President and Founder of Global Policy Solutions, noted, "[A] considerable amount of business gets done in the social arena and many times people make decisions based on how much they like you." Since likeability can help your career advancement, being positive will always help get you further than negativity. Another critical reason for taking a positive approach at work is that it will make you a more solution-focused employee. Denise Incandela, President of Saks Direct at Saks Fifth Avenue, reflected, "I'm a 'glass half-full' kind of person; I try to be positive and as a result, solution-oriented. That has always served me very well."

If you put yourself in the shoes of a manager, would you rather supervise an employee that bemoans their work and points out every flaw in the company, or an employee who comes up with new solutions and strives to make improvements? There is no contest between the two, right? Of course, it is much easier to be positive when you like what you do for a living and have basic competence in your role. If you find that you are becoming increasingly negative at work, it is your responsibility to remove yourself from the situation by looking for a new job, or at the very least, exploring what is underlying your negative mindset.

THE VIP TREATMENT

One of the best ways to channel your positive, can-do work philosophy is to take an internal customer service approach with those you work with. Internal customer service means serving those in your organization just as well as you would serve your best customer. I recommend that you actually view your coworkers as customers—without regard to their title, rank, or hierarchy.

So few people actually go above and beyond in their work, that the few people who provide "service with a smile" tend to stand out and get noticed. If you gain a reputation for delivering strong results with a great attitude, it will be hard for management *not* to get word of it! Whether that translates to a promotion, a high profile project you get to manage, or a new mentor for you to learn from, it is worth the effort. Taking an internal customer service approach will also model for those around you, including any subordinates, how things should get done. Even if you are the first to do it at your company, you are starting the positive momentum of change that your organization needs.

A WORD ON OFFERING A HAND

Part of succeeding on the job is teamwork, a trait that I would encourage any up-and-comer to possess and demonstrate. Whether you recognize when others are overwhelmed and offer to help, take the time to teach a new employee a process, or fill in at the last minute for someone who cannot attend a meeting, demonstrating that you are team-oriented will always reflect positively on you.

Being helpful is important for many reasons. First, it is the right thing to do if you have the time, bandwidth, and ability. Second, it will help fortify your work alliances, broadening the circle of people who will help you when you need a favor returned one day. Third, you may learn new skills or gain new exposure as a result of helping someone on a project. Autumn Bayles pointed out, "I don't hear people volunteer to help on projects that much. Lots of opportunities are handed to us all the time so jump in and show that you're proactive and eager. Make things easy for others." Helpfulness can emphasize that you are hungry to grow, eager to learn, and cooperative.

All signs point to the fact that being helpful is a winning career strategy, right? Wrong. There is one area where being helpful is not, well, helpful. There is a certain "helpfulness" that many women feel hardwired to demonstrate, derived from our socialization and the historical role women have played in corporate America. When it comes to lowly, support-type tasks, I see women volunteering to be "helpful" by offering to take on administrative to-dos, even when it is not their job. As an example—over the two years that I attended business school, my fellow students and I often met in teams in which we would discuss our projects and then circulate notes for all to refer to later. Although all members of the team participated in the meetings, one person would always volunteer to take notes. Ninety percent of the time, I noticed that a woman offered to do it.

This started to bother me, and what bothered me most was that I noticed I fell into the same habit! Since, historically speaking, women have been the ones to fetch coffee, take notes, type, or play a support role administratively, it is not far-fetched to posit that both men and women may naturally look to women to fulfill these duties, out of habit. Be aware of this when you attend meetings, both in yourself and others. Consider biting your tongue the next time you feel compelled to get the visitor coffee, take notes at a meeting, or get your manager that document he or she left behind in his or her office. Lending a hand to others is kind; however, do not perpetuate a stereotype by instinctively taking on support tasks. Doing so can position you in the eyes of leaders as that "helpful Admin" rather than the "future Manager" that you want to be seen as.

Shannon S. S. Herzfeld, Vice President of Government Relations at Archer Daniels Midland Company, supported this idea, "Ask the tough business questions. Many younger women want to be helpful and nice rather than portraying themselves as someone who grows the bottom line." How do you want to be seen? Are you always the note taker, assistant, or gofer? Consider selectively where and how you want to be helpful. Personally, I like to engage in mentoring as a way to be "helpful," by offering good ideas, best practices, and suggestions to more junior employees. As a result, I put my energies into helping other people get their jobs done and I no longer blindly volunteer to always be the note taker!

MAKE MEETINGS COUNT

We are often judged on our performance based on day-to-day interactions at work, not just the project results we deliver. Meetings are one form of this day-to-day interaction, where our participation counts and will surely be judged. An important aspect of attending meetings is deciding that you will be an active participant. To convey that you are a leader-in-training, get comfortable taking a stand in these forums. Karen Holbrook, Ph.D., Vice President of Research and Innovation at University of South Florida and immediate past president of Ohio State University, recalled, "When I was young I wouldn't always speak up when I had something to say. Speak out and offer your position. It's better to be a participant than just a listener."

DeeDee Wilson takes this one step further. You can be better prepared for meetings, she noted, if you decide how you will contribute ahead of time. DeeDee shared, "My coach told me once that I should always know who I'm going to be in each meeting—whether the decision-maker, the note-taker, or the input-giver. This was great advice because now I ask myself that before each meeting, which helps me to prepare accordingly." You may want to mimic DeeDee's practice by identifying what role you will play *before* entering a meeting. If you are unclear, you may want to start the meeting by asking the meeting's facilitator, "How can I serve you best in this meeting? Are you looking for input, help with a decision, or to just share information with the group?" Asking these clarifying questions shows that you want to make the best contribution possible, and more often than not, other meeting attendees will be glad you asked.

GETTING, TAKING, AND GIVING CREDIT

Over the years, I have noticed a distinct difference between men and women's tendency to take credit for achievements. While I have witnessed numerous male associates assume credit for projects they have led—as they beam with pride, I observe many fewer women doing so. This tendency for women to downplay achievements is most likely rooted in several factors, one of which could be a fear of coming across as arrogant or self-serving. It is also clear that boys and girls are socialized differently when it comes to achievements. Research shows that growing up, boys and girls are praised differently and for different achievements. This conditioning translates to the workplace as conditioned kids become adult workers. This is evidenced by studies conducted by Madeline E. Heilman. One of Heilman's studies found that when men and women collaborate on a work task, especially a stereotypically "male" task that draws on decisiveness and leadership, men and women observing the study participants both placed less value on the woman's contribution relative to the man's (Winerman, 2005). This finding points to the fact that women's work contributions may be undervalued to begin with. Clearly, not taking credit for accomplishments only further hinders a woman's value and ability to get recognized.

One way that women tend to dilute their noteworthy achievements is by starting sentences with "we" rather than "I" when talking about an achievement. By using the term "we," observers have no idea who came up with the idea, who led the effort, or who did the lion's share of work. An easy way to solve this problem is to be clear about who led, managed, or spearheaded a project. By keeping things fact-based, no one can effectively contest or second-guess your claim. Additionally, it leaves little room for confusion as to who is "owed" credit. An example of giving yourself credit might be, "I'm really pleased to see the progress made on the company's strategic plan. Last year, when I suggested we update our plan, I never thought it would lead us to such a major overhaul. The effort required was comprehensive, and many stakeholders were involved. I am extremely proud of our final work product."

It is equally important to give specific credit to others as it is to report on your own achievements. Reporting on the facts also lessens politics and perceptions of favoritism. An example of effectively giving credit to another would be, "I'd just like to take a minute to recognize Julie for her work on the Simpson account. Julie has been instrumental in managing the day-to-day logistics of the account's operations. She has overseen the account management without a single hitch, which is no small feat considering how many details there are."

Along with giving and taking credit, a noteworthy data point emerged in the interviews I conducted. All of the women I interviewed were able to take ownership for their successes. They talked about what they were proudest of accomplishing and truly owned their triumphs. While they credited people in their lives for giving support, they truly owned the changes and improvements that they uniquely made at work. This pattern points to the fact that all of us, even if we are not top executives, must acknowledge and share our achievements.

Where could you take credit more often? How can you take credit without being overbearing or bragging? Where credit is involved, communication is essential. You can convey your contributions by communicating with your boss, as often as weekly, to keep him or her abreast of your accomplishments. You can also take opportunities in meetings and brainstorms to give yourself and others due credit. Follow-up emails after meetings are another good way of reiterating or summarizing your ideas and keeping them associated with you. Summarizing the importance of self-promotion, Jamie McCourt, President of the Los Angeles Dodgers, noted, "I have been in several situations where I offered up an idea, and the credit for the idea was given to a man. It's one thing if a woman doesn't get credit, but it's another if someone else gets credit for her idea!"

RELATIONSHIP BEFORE TASK

When I asked Cuc T. Vu, Chief Diversity Officer at Human Rights Campaign, what competencies made her promotable, she replied, "I always put relationship before task. I see people as being most important. I realize that even though it's easy to get stuck in everyday work tasks, people need nourishing." Cuc's eloquent sentiment was reinforced throughout my interviews. Women, who are natural relationship builders and relationship maintainers, can use this natural ability as they train for leadership. Jeanine Becker, Senior Counsel at Motorola, Inc., reinforced, "More and more, the business world is shifting toward leveraged relationships. These relationships have a real impact on the bottom line, and women excel at focusing on these relationships."

Regardless of the type of industry you work in, relationships matter. Reflecting on her leadership tenure, Roxanne Spillett, President and CEO of Boys and Girls Clubs of America, shared, "The older I get, the more I realize just how key relationships are to a nonprofit. Whether its board members, counterparts, donors, service delivery staff or recipients of services, strong relationships are vital."

Mitigating team adversity and helping others work through conflict is one more requirement of a good leader. Dominique Schurman, Chief Executive Officer of Papyrus, advised, "The higher up you go in a hierarchy, the more management is about bringing people together and getting them to work effectively. It becomes less about how much technical expertise you have. This is an area where women are naturals, bringing the best out of a team and getting them to work well together."

PEOPLE MANAGEMENT

When it comes to managing employees, many books, courses, and seminars exist to teach those who are new to supervision. There has also been considerable research done on what employees want from their leaders. The research of Kouzes and Posner, for example, shows that there is a set of characteristics that followers consistently look for in a leader. People most often want leaders who are honest, forward looking, competent, and inspiring. In their book *The Leadership Challenge*, Kouzes and Posner (2007) go on to say that credibility is "the foundation of leadership." If credibility is indeed marked by honesty, a future orientation, competence, and inspiration, how does one earn such distinction?

Research and other resources can be extremely helpful as a general roadmap for managing others; however, there is really no replacement for firsthand experience. Maya Rockeymoore shared, "You can study managing or leading, but there's no substitute for doing it. You can prepare by asking for more responsibility and seeking out these kinds of opportunities outside of your job. In my own career, Congressman Charles Rangel made me his Chief of Staff at the age of 26, which was an incredible opportunity to learn about managing an office and people. I also made it a point to get in leadership positions in college."

A major part of leading and managing others is finding your own management style. Your unique style is often born out of the good and bad bosses you yourself have had, and many other nuanced personal factors. Denise Incandela reflected on her own experience learning to manage others. She noted, "I wish I had known the value of building working relationships earlier on. When I first finished my MBA, I was more self-centered than I am now. Now I ask myself if I'm inspiring a 'followership' of direct reports, peers, and senior management. If I'm not, then I need to change my behavior. I also ask myself, 'Am I developing my direct reports enough? Am I showing them I care about them?' In building relationships, you have to give a lot." The task of managing others is complex, subjective, and dynamic. It can take a considerable amount of energy and investment, and, of course, it will never be a perfect "science" given that it involves human beings.

One strategy that has proven helpful for Dominique Schurman is transparency. Dominique shared, "I try not to let my ego get in the way. I'm honest with my own team about my abilities and weaknesses, and try to create an environment where people don't have to be perfect. It's key to be honest if you don't know the answer to something and seek out advice and input from others." Many managers believe that as holders of vital information, they should keep it to themselves. True leaders, as opposed to managers, are open with information and solicit upward and downward feedback. Can you think of other differences between managers and leaders? Table 3.2 contains some of the most distinct differences to come out of the interviews I did.

Table 3.2   Manager versus Leadership Traits

Manager	Leader
Task oriented	Relationship oriented
Keeper of information	Transparent with information
Needs power	Empowers others
Acknowledges and works within limits	Envisions what could be
Creates rules; hands-on	Removes barriers; hands-off
Gets work done	Keeps people engaged
Transactional	Transformational
Focused on the here and now	Focused on the future
Focuses on technical skills	Focuses on motivational skills
Dictatorial, authoritative	Inspiring, influencing
Position in the hierarchy	Level of influence

When considering her own leadership style, Cathy Fleming, Partner at Nixon Peabody LLP, shared, "I am an effective motivator, [a] good consensus-builder, and a strong delegator. I trust people to carry out their tasks and I recognize the value of getting buy-in from people. I've been able to refine these skills through experiences like being a Chief at the U.S. Attorney's Office, President of the National Association for Women in Law (NAWL), and as the Chair of a law department in a law firm." What groups, projects, or jobs could provide you with more opportunities to lead and manage others? If you do supervise others, what is your current approach—management or leadership?

KNOWING YOUR STRENGTHS AND WEAKNESSES

Openness to feedback, on our best and weakest qualities, is another hallmark of the women executives that I interviewed. Autumn Bayles reflected, "People prefer a down-to-earth leader, not a dictatorial leader. I would recommend asking others how they perceive you. This can be hard to do because sometimes you don't want to know the answer. After I ask my direct reports to evaluate their strengths and weaknesses in performance reviews, I always ask them to evaluate me the same way." Far too few leaders ask for upward feedback. Doing so makes employees feel respected and included, and paves the way for ongoing honest, two-way dialogue.

Karen Holbrook cautioned against overanalyzing ourselves, however. She commented, "Many of us look at ourselves too critically. We can stand to take less blame and be slightly less analytical. Overall though, listen to cues, and be very open because people will generally tell you what you are and aren't good at. Make sure that you're not seen as a 'good-news' person only. People have to know that you can take some constructive criticism." Many formal mechanisms exist to help with identifying strengths and weaknesses. A few of the most common assessments available to professionals are explored below.

A 360-DEGREE VIEW

Assessments such as 360-degree tools encourage an understanding of how you are viewed by others. This kind of assessment is always done in the workplace, usually in the form of a survey, and is named to reflect the holistic approach it takes to employee performance—where an individual is assessed from all angles. Performance feedback for an individual is gathered from a supervisor, peers, direct reports, and sometimes even customers. Additionally, 360-degree assessments require that participants take their own self-assessment, evaluating what they see as their strengths and weaknesses. Focusing heavily on behaviors, 360-degree assessments are an invaluable tool for identifying one's "blind spots," those areas that require improvement and are not necessarily readily obvious. This process also illuminates strengths and opportunities for growth that participants do not readily recognize in themselves.

At the conclusion of the survey and data collection process, a participant usually receives a data report and an interpretation session with an internal or external coach. Perhaps the most helpful aspect of the reporting process, a participant can see how they rated their skill levels compared to the data provided by the other raters, or rater team. A gap analysis can then be performed so you can see where your own perceptions are different (for better or worse) than your coworkers.

While it is common for such assessments to elicit an emotional response, a woman who wants to secure a high-ranking position should take advantage of all opportunities for self-learning available to her. The women I interviewed noted that the process of "being assessed" only intensifies as one gets more senior in her career, so the act of looking in the mirror should be a continual one, and be seen as an ongoing exercise in learning. Mind you, self-reflection is not about striving for perfection, but gathering insights and honing your ability to change directions if you are on the wrong path.

COMPETENCY ASSESSMENTS

Competency assessments are most often offered through workplaces, with the goal of encouraging growth among participants and the company. Competency assessments are developed based on certain career paths, roles or job descriptions. The most needed skills, behavior, and knowledge are identified for a given job and a model and survey are developed. Often administered by HR departments or outside consulting firms, competency assessments help organizations to understand where the knowledge and skills reside in strategic functions, so that the company can more precisely staff projects, spread knowledge from seasoned employees to those who are junior, and help plan for employee succession.

Competency assessments provide excellent "self-reflection" benefits to individuals as well. While competency assessments almost always require you to rate yourself, these assessments do not necessarily require ratings from others. Competency assessments provide excellent data on where an employee is developmentally, and what skills could help them do their job more effectively. The results of the assessments can help a participant justify a training investment in an area of weakness, show evidence for a needed promotion, and spur actions such as being assigned a mentor.

ANNUAL PERFORMANCE REVIEWS

The annual performance review, while discussed more fully in Chapter 6, is certainly an ample opportunity for self-reflection. An event that usually occurs 1–2 times per year, performance reviews are dreaded by many, but provide fertile ground for pinpointing your strengths and weaknesses and learning how others perceive you. Performance reviews work best when they take the form of an open, two-way conversation, not a one-side lecture.

Perhaps their greatest asset, performance reviews give employees the chance to ask and answer the question, "How am I creating value for the organization?" Similarly, they give managers the chance to answer the question, "How are we investing in this employee and positioning her for success?"

One of the most important things you can do before a review is to show your boss that you have done some amount of reflecting before walking into the meeting. Many performance reviews include a self-assessment component. Even if yours does not, honestly appraise your performance over time and note for yourself where you have thrived, succeeded, struggled, challenged yourself, and most of all—what value you have created for the organization. Remember that "value" for the organization can take many forms. You may have created value by giving a client or customer a positive experience, by managing a project so successfully that you received accolades or praise from management, by saving the company money through an efficiency or improvement you proposed, or by surpassing a job-related metric given to you. You also may have created value for the organization by helping to quickly get new team members up to speed, serving on an internal task force or going the extra mile in some way.

If you have had more than one job where you have received a performance review, you should actively look for patterns and themes in the feedback you receive. This lets you know what competencies are dominant or natural for you and what is a less natural skill or behavior. While some feedback can be difficult to hear, keeping a nondefensive attitude will serve you best. If you want more clarity on a strength or weakness that your boss shares with you, you can ask for specific examples or explain that you would like to better understand what your boss means. Like any process built for reflection, you will get out of a performance review what you put into it. Be open to the process, honestly appraise yourself ahead of time, and be a full participant.

MAKE YOUR CAREER INTENTIONS KNOWN

Annual performance reviews represent a great time to do something many women overlook: making your career intentions known. All too often, women neglect to share where they want to be, including the specific position they would like to have. Yet, telling your boss and other individuals of power and influence about your goals can land you exactly where you want to be. Alexandra Miller urged, "Don't be shy about telling those above you that you're ambitious and want more from life." Remember, people are handicapped in their ability to guide opportunities and promotions your way if they do not know what you want! Ask for what you want, and get comfortable telling your boss where you want to be.

INFORMAL FEEDBACK

Get in the habit of asking for feedback following developmental opportunities—whether or not they seem significant. Remember that meetings, presentations, and client dealings are all examples of excellent learning opportunities. Following interactions like these, be sure to ask one or two people in attendance for feedback. These should be people you respect, who are either at your own level or those that have the kind of role you would like to secure.

I have learned the hard way that it is important to be direct and explicit in asking for balanced feedback. If you truly want both positive and negative input, you need to request it. An interesting phenomenon, when you ask people if they have any feedback, they will tend to give you negative feedback only, even if they believe you did several things well. For this reason, and because I am a strong proponent of identifying and leveraging your areas of strength, I suggest you ask for both types of input. Knowledge of what you did and did not do well will help you solidify your career and make informed choices. Solicit balanced feedback by saying, "What do you think I did well in there, and where could I have managed things better?" or "Tell me two things I did well in that presentation and two things I could improve upon."

This continuous practice will have numerous benefits. For one, it thickens your skin. Learning to handle constructive feedback truly is a skill, and one that gets easier with time, experience, and practice. Asking for feedback outside of your annual review shows that you are hungry to learn and grow, and willing to reflect on and improve yourself. Asking for feedback is especially helpful if you have a boss that is not communicative or quick to share his or her opinions with you. Consider the act of asking for feedback a lifelong exercise. Regardless of what success you attain, there will be learning waiting for you around every corner. Vicki Ho suggests, "When people are successful, they feel infallible—but no matter what your level, you have to keep getting and hearing feedback."

DELIVERY AND FOLLOW-THROUGH

Despite whom you know, how you present yourself, and the way you speak, nothing says "take me seriously" like strong delivery of your work. Being seen as a strong performer who can be consistently relied upon gives you credibility and favorable standing. Substantiating this thinking, a reputation for dependable, well-executed work emerged as a hallmark of the leaders I interviewed. Denise Incandela reiterated this idea, citing, "Good relationships with my bosses and a focus on over-delivering have helped me succeed. I am also hard working, prepared, tenacious, and passionate about what I do." While there are many wonderful strategies you can employ to fast-track your career, remember that executing your daily work tasks well should be a "constant."

YOUR CAREER IS YOURS ALONE—RUN WITH IT!

While you can strategize many different ways to succeed on the job, success is more of mindset than anything else. There are small and large ways that we can learn to be leaders, and many opportunities are more readily available to us than we realize. Roxanne Spillett notes, "An informal way to get training is to look at every interaction as an opportunity to learn. Every meeting or dealing you encounter with a successful man or woman is a chance to learn. See group interactions or meetings as an opportunity to wear two hats: one as observer/learner, and one as participant." Roxanne went on to say, "Right in front of us are all kinds of opportunities for learning about leadership. Everyday interactions provide big opportunities to grow professionally and personally."

There are endless career strategies available for you and your experimentation. You are 100% in charge of your career growth, opportunities, and success. By taking full responsibility for where your career is, you can drive change and plot a course of action. Melissa M. Monk underscores this idea noting, "Your career doesn't just happen. I wish I'd known how much you have to drive your own career growth. Plan it, work it, and revise it. No one else will own your development and career, so you need to."

4
Networking for a Lifetime

WHO YOU KNOW MATTERS

For many people, networking conjures up negative images of mindless social chatter, forced mingling, or a meaningless exchange of business cards. The truth about networking, however, is that it can lead to career advancement in ways one simply cannot achieve elsewhere. Leveraging "who you know" is something aspiring leaders need to do whether they are looking for a job or if they have already secured one. What's more, nearly every woman I interviewed credited networking as having helped her career growth. "People" were often cited as a reason that the interviewees were able to advance, particularly when they identified a mentor or group, or had some kind of champion advocating for their advancement. Networking provides opportunities for learning, meeting people, broadening your thinking, and connecting to new jobs and career resources. While networking does require a time commitment, it can yield significant dividends for you and your organization.

One benefit of engaging in networking is that it can help women to create a more level playing field in comparison to male counterparts. Many interviewees I spoke with said that men have historically had more networks in the workplace than women. Patricia Deyton, Director of the Center for Gender in Organizations at Simmons School of Management, reinforced this point, "Networking can help women a lot but we're not 'there' yet. Men have much stronger informal networks than women do." Similarly, Shannon S. S. Herzfeld, Vice President of Government Relations at Archer Daniels Midland Company, reflected on this topic noting, "Women don't have the same kind of fraternity in businesses that men do. Looking at my own experience, often times I did not have the same number of personal ties that my peers had to the boss." Since organizations are run largely by men, most corporate networks are created and "maintained" by men. Vicki Ho, General Manager, Asia Services for GE Healthcare Clinical Services at General Electric, took this idea a step further, noting how networks provide a measure of resilience. Vicki shared, "Men have cohorts of other men to help them survive political blood baths—women should create networks so they have similar support."

Substantiating this point, research suggests that men see networking as more instrumental to their career success than women do. In 2008, for example, Accenture released a report entitled *One Step Ahead of 2011: A New Horizon for Working Women,* which highlighted a survey of over 4,000 male and female business professionals in North America, South America, Europe, and Asia. The study looked at numerous workplace factors, one of which was career advancement. While women were more likely than men to attribute their career advancement to ambition and drive, passion for their chosen careers, and family support, men more often cited technical capabilities and fostering professional relationships as having helped their career advancement (2008). Women, who are "naturals" at building relationships, can reap rewards by leveraging those relationships more often. Supporting this idea was Karen Holbrook, Ph.D., Vice President of Research and Innovation at University of South Florida and immediate past president of Ohio State University, who said, "I don't care what area you work in, who you know makes a difference. Having broad networks allows you to help yourself—as well as others, and the latter becomes more important the more senior you get and want to help your junior colleagues."

TYPES OF NETWORKING

Networking can be formal or informal, planned or spontaneous, and done in a group or with a single person. Formal networking groups exist in many varieties and have different expectations of their members. These groups are typically forums intended for professional development and relationship building, and have some kind of stated criteria for membership. Professional groups can be industry-specific, for example, Women in Aerospace or the American Medical Women's Association, or role-specific, for instance, the Society of Women Engineers or the National Association of Women Lawyers. Still other networking groups center on a particular cause, such as humanitarian efforts, animal rights, or equal pay for women. Groups can be housed in universities and colleges, corporations, or nonprofit organizations, or they can operate totally independently. Some networking efforts are convened at large conferences, others in smaller weekly or monthly events.

Networking also constitutes the alliance building that you do one-on-one with people. These interactions can take place in everyday forums such as meetings or can be totally unstructured and unplanned. For example, networking can be as simple as running into someone you've heard is a top performer at your organization and saying something like, "I've heard so many impressive things about you. I'd love to offer you my help if you need a hand on a project. It would be great to collaborate and learn from you." Think of your networking activities as casting a wide net inclusive of people, groups, and causes with which you have a genuine inclination or connection.

BENEFITS OF NETWORKING

Why bother networking anyway? For one, networking can help to keep you motivated, aware of current trends in your business, and connected to those who have your dream job or key contacts. It can help you to identify your professional blind spots, assumptions, and barriers to success. Good networks provide a learning environment devoid of pressure or judgment, and foster openness among members. Cathy Fleming, Partner at Nixon Peabody LLP, discussed networking with me, citing, "Networking is essential. . . . This includes your own network (colleagues and friends) and organized networks. The National Association of Women Lawyers is a wonderful networking community that has helped me—and others—tremendously. This kind of organization encourages you to keep asking yourself, 'Where do I want to be in ten years?' and 'What skills do I need to get there?'" Cathy's point is a good one; there is an added measure of accountability in networking groups that can give members a gentle push when they are stagnating, helping to keep their ambitions alive.

LOCATING JOB OPPORTUNITIES

Beyond their ability to help you develop personally, networks can give you access to professional opportunities that you may not otherwise hear about. Autumn Bayles, Senior Vice President of Strategic Operations at Tasty Baking Company, commented, "I think networking with other women is helpful to build confidence, get insights from peers, and have a sounding board. I furthered my career through networks—in fact, I found out about my current job through my MBA network. Without that network, I probably wouldn't have found out about the opportunity." Networks can make you aware of unpublished or new job opportunities, internships, special projects, or volunteer jobs. Networks also build the number of people that are vested in your success. The amazing thing about finding professional opportunities through your network is that you are hearing about them through the very people who are likely to endorse you. What more could you ask for?

BRANDING

Networking can also help you develop and strengthen your personal brand. At its essence, branding is about conveying the unique combination of capabilities that you, as an individual, possess. Tom Peter's landmark 1997 article "The Brand Called You," featured in *Fast Company* magazine, uncovered this emergent trend. Said Peters, "Regardless of age, regardless of position, regardless of the business we happen to be in . . . our most important job is to be head marketer for the brand called You." The women I interviewed supported this idea, pointing out that at its core, personal branding is about self-awareness and ownership of your potential. Networks help with branding, as they open you up to new feedback sources, many times from those more seasoned than you. This allows you to get guidance on your key differentiators, presence, and image—all in a safe learning environment. Women can leverage their participation in networks as a means to owning and promoting successes and distinctive personal capabilities. Then, they can confidently seek out more experiences that lead to greater professional growth and fulfillment.

NETWORKS HELP YOU WITH PLAN B

Perhaps the most compelling reason for engaging in networking is that it can safeguard your career. Whether you face the backdrop of an economic downturn, corporate downsizing, or you need to escape a downright miserable job situation, networking can help you to be more resilient. When asked how young women can best leverage their networks, Vicki Ho advised, "Create a network where you can become known by people other than just your immediate boss. This networking group can eventually vouch for you. Being liked by all your company's senior leaders is not necessarily in your control, but making yourself known in networking groups is." Vicki's insightful comment elucidates that regardless of the threats to your job, getting out and networking makes good business sense. Vicki went on to say, "In this day of reorganizations, you can work your butt off at a company and still find yourself out of work one day. Having a broader circle can help you recover quickly. Having a network will also help if your boss is not supportive, or if they are threatened by someone young and up-and-coming."

FINDING AND TEST-DRIVING GROUPS

The best way to find a network depends on what you want to get out of the group. For example, are you looking to connect with international, national, regional, or local contacts? Similarly, do you want to be better networked within your industry, role, or function? You might also ask yourself if it is a certain skill, topic, or cause in which you are interested. Once you know, loosely speaking, whom you want to connect with, you can begin by reaching out to those around you. This existing network might be comprised of those in your organization or alma mater, or you can informally survey those you know to see where they network and which groups they benefit most from. Referrals and testimonials are a great way to learn about groups you might not otherwise hear about. You can also search online for key terms that interest you. For example, I searched Google using the words "women," "business," and "association" to find an organization I am now a part of—the National Association of Women MBAs.

Consider the story of Jeanette, a client of mine who sought out and successfully engaged in a networking group. Jeanette was looking for a public speaking group. She was hungry to move up at her company and specifically wanted to become a vice president. She knew that the vice presidents in her organization were called upon often to speak in public forums. Jeanette had little experience with public speaking, but figured that if she could find a way to practice public speaking, she would most likely improve her skill level. Jeanette consulted colleagues and friends and was ultimately referred to Toastmasters International, a nonprofit organization committed to helping people become more competent and comfortable in front of an audience.

Jeanette located a local chapter online, began attending weekly meetings, and even took on a minor volunteer role with the group as a coordinator. She found Toastmasters to be a perfect match for her needs given that other network members had the exact same goal as she had— to get more comfortable with and build their skills in public speaking. In particular, she noted value in being able to "stumble and fall with this group" and yet bring her best learning into the workplace. Jeanette liked the fact that she could learn in a protected environment, free of coworkers and higher ups at her company. She ultimately learned a lot from her experience with the group and practiced numerous speeches over her time as a member. Jeanette shares that the group helped her hone her communication skills, but that the added benefits of increased confidence and a more effective leadership presence were pleasant surprises.

Clearly, it makes sense to look for a group that can provide you with additional value or promise. Rosslyn Kleeman, Chair of the Coalition for

Effective Change, shares an important criterion for selecting a group, "Whichever network you join, the group needs to match your style and your values." Regardless of the networking group you find, you will get—and most likely give—more to the experience if there is a genuine match between your values and interests and those of the group. How do you know if there is a match in your values? You can begin by asking what the values of the company are, and probing as to how the organization lives them. You can also ask about the mission, vision for the future, and strategic goals of the organization, as they should be an indicator of values. Lastly, getting out there and actually participating in a group is a good way to know if there is a value match. Doing so will help you gain insights that you will not learn by simply checking an organization's Web site or doing research.

It is more than acceptable to seek out a group, test-drive it, and decide it is right or wrong for you. In fact, I would encourage you to do that. The key, however, is if you find you have a mismatch, you will want to consider how to exit gracefully. If a group is wrong for you, either because of the culture fit, time commitment, or activities of the group, make sure that you feel like you have given the group an ample chance. Consider explaining, in constructive but noncritical terms, why you want to leave to the group's leader or membership representative. Doing so will ensure that you do not burn any bridges or get an unfavorable reputation in your industry. Networks and communities of practice are often small worlds, where the same people continually circulate. If you need to leave a group, by all means, do so—but in a way that preserves your legacy positively.

ETIQUETTE

Believe it or not, there is a certain etiquette of networking that should not be underestimated. When joining a network, a member often has expectations of the group, but the group also has expectations of the member. An actively engaged member shows her commitment to the group, which can position her for more formal leadership roles within the group and help her get the most learning out of a network.

The very best forum is one in which a professional woman has a natural interest or inclination; joining networks just for the sake of listing them on a résumé is an anti-advancement strategy. While it may be tempting to bolster your résumé by joining as many groups as possible, try to select a few networks that will add value and to which you can contribute most. Whatever the scope of your interactions with a group, consider how you can leave with a positive reputation.

WHY ENGAGE IN A WOMEN-ONLY NETWORK?

Social psychology tells us that similarity is a significant factor in encouraging interaction. If this is the case, women may not look to male management as readily for help or advice as they would female management. Since similarity and interaction mutually reinforce each other, it makes sense that women may find comfort convening with, or at the very least, having access to, others that are like them. Cuc T. Vu, Chief Diversity Officer at Human Rights Campaign, illustrates this point, noting, "Women can have self-doubts, low expectations, and fear of failure, and I think because of that, we take comfort in each other's company. I think especially for minority women, there is comfort is seeing your self mirrored in a mentor." Since women largely see more men than women in management positions, they may internalize the lack of female presence and assume that striving for leadership is somehow unrealistic. The mere act of convening with women at all levels of your organization, industry, or functional group can build confidence, helping to solidify your belief that leadership is indeed a plausible career path.

Numerous women I interviewed suggested that taking on a formal role within a networking group helped grow their leadership skills and deepen their connection with a networking group. There are so many ways to get involved with networking organizations and positions with these groups are abundant. Keep in mind that assignments serving with a group can be quite varied; some are ongoing while others are singular. Formal roles can be substantive, such as handling the finances of the group, while others involve coordinating a one-time event, for instance a bake sale. If you do not hear about roles in a group, do not be afraid to make it known that you would like a formal role in a given area if and when one becomes available. Most organizations are happy to get an offer for help.

ONLINE NETWORKING GROUPS

Networking online, which has mushroomed in popularity, can be highly beneficial and convenient, and can save you significant time traveling to in-person events. Online networking connects you virtually with others, allowing you to share ideas, information, and common interests. While online networking has some conveniences not offered by in-person events, it still requires a time commitment and a conscientious approach to cultivating and maintaining relationships. Depending on what you want to get out of your online networks, you can designate your time to activities accordingly. In other words, if you want to be seen as an expert on a subject, or further promote your personal brand, company, or expertise, you may want to take a different approach than someone who just wants to connect with people at a certain company where they would like to get a job.

If you join more than one online networking site, you may want to consider diversifying the sites to which you belong. While many sites such as LinkedIn, Doostang, Jigsaw, and Spoke are professionally focused, more socially focused sites, for instance AfterCollege, Facebook, and MySpace, also exist. Some online networking communities are international, while others are region-specific or local. Take Nadine's use of online networking as an example. Nadine is a banking executive in Indianapolis, Indiana, and is a member of LinkedIn as well as SmallerIndiana, an online networking community for professionals at the local level in Indiana. Nadine says she gets benefit from SmallerIndiana because she can easily meet members for coffee and can do business development in person. She likes that LinkedIn gives her a different perspective, however, where she can find leaders from around the country based on the Web site's search tools. Being part of the two different groups allows Nadine to grow her network locally and nationally.

LinkedIn, one of the most widely used professional Web sites, is a favorite given how simple it is to use. One can easily join subgroups on the Web site, for example, San Francisco Accountants, U.S. Career Consultants, or alumni clubs of former employers, for instance, GE or Booz Allen Hamilton. Many groups are open to all users and give you access to individuals you would not otherwise have the opportunity to meet. Some online communities require a fee; however, I recommend trying their basic, free package before you pay for anything to see if you like it. I have personally found more than enough uses for LinkedIn using the standard, free package.

I have also found it very beneficial to use LinkedIn for getting and giving professional recommendations. Particularly if you are leaving a company and want to stay in touch with a boss or a colleague, or have met someone that you want to keep a connection with, online networking sites are a great way to do this. At a minimum, networking sites can serve as an electronic rolodex, where you not only have access to your contacts, but also your contacts' contacts. If you want greater involvement, you can show your level of expertise in an area by answering public questions and getting your answers rated favorably by others. You can also consider writing a blog or starting a discussion forum.

Regardless of what online activity you engage in, make sure that you are projecting a professional image of yourself. When we discussed this topic, Alexandra Miller, Chief Executive Officer of Mercedes Medical, Inc., advised, "Clean up your Facebook, LinkedIn, and MySpace accounts if you have them. Create them if you don't." Many online activities you engage in can have a long life. Do not post or say anything that you would not be comfortable telling your office over a loud speaker.

NETWORKING INTERNALLY

The truth is many of us do not take the time to include in our networks those people we see or work with everyday. Around us are many talented individuals with helpful connections who we forget to utilize. How can you combat this? For one, make your networking interests known at work. I was once standing in a corporate lunchroom while someone was describing her idea for a book to a friend. The woman was lamenting that she wanted to bounce her book idea off someone in the publishing industry but had no contacts. A young man walked into the kitchen, overhead the conversation and offered to connect the woman with someone he knew at Random House. The woman was not just referred to *someone* in publishing, she was referred to an influential editor at one of the best publishing houses in the country. Many times people you interact with every day have colleagues, friends, and other acquaintances that could help you and your career.

Another aspect of internal networking is represented in the social area. Happy hours and after-hours gatherings can give you access to people you do not know or work closely with, can help make friends, and can provide vital information on your organization's culture. Erin McGinnis, National Committee Chair of the Society of Women Engineers, reflected, "I think it's critical to network. I just went to a work-related happy hour recently where my colleagues and I discussed how often women opt out of such events. The problem with missing those events is that you're left out from hearing stories of how people have overcome organizational obstacles, and what new job opportunities exist. I've always made time for networking whether through formal groups or even through LinkedIn.com and it's helped me." Erin's point about learning how to traverse organizational obstacles through networks is an excellent one. Social activities with colleagues may give you the information you need to get support for a change, work effectively with a difficult person, or get noticed by key individuals.

CORPORATE AFFINITY GROUPS

Numerous groups have been formed at large corporations, often called *affinity groups,* where members share a key characteristic such as gender, race, or a minority status. The fact that the group shares a similarity can be helpful in terms of identifying with others, finding a common bond, and learning from others' lessons and experiences. Joining a corporate affinity group can be especially helpful if you are new to a company and need to learn about the culture of your organization. Through such groups, you can get invaluable insights into the unspoken rules of the organization's culture and gain a sense of belonging.

ALUMNI CLUBS

Some companies are very creative about networking with their alumni or past employees. Organizations such as Boston Consulting Group and Booz Allen Hamilton have designed innovative programs to stay connected to their alumni workers, either through surveys, networking events, or online portals. Reengaging former employees can generate new clients for the employer and reengage past employees who might want to rejoin the organization. There are significant benefits for individuals as well. Without making a long-term commitment, an alumni can come back to the company on a project or part-time basis, learn about new opportunities or directions the company is taking, and most of all reconnect with many of the people in his or her network, benefiting from the growth others' individual networks have seen.

SPONTANEOUS NETWORKING

We tend to think of networking opportunities happening through groups, associations, tradeshows, conferences, and other speaking engagements. There are also less formal networking opportunities, however, that can provide you with equally as helpful information or support. While you set about planning for high-impact, meaningful networking opportunities, do not forget to leave yourself open to spontaneous opportunities as well. Consider the example of one of my clients, Alyse:

Alyse, a marketing consultant, attended a national conference where her company had a display on exhibition. Her job was to promote her company, manage the display, answer people's questions, and collect new leads for her company. All conference guests were invited to attend the midday luncheon in a large ballroom. Alyse sat next to a friendly woman whom she talked easily with throughout the luncheon. While Alyse and her contact had a lot in common personally, they began to realize that a partnership or at the very least a collaboration between their companies would be of major benefit. The companies offered similar services, but had gaps in their offerings where the other company had particularly strong competencies. Once back at the office, Elyse presented an idea for a partnership to her firm, got approval, and was given responsibility for managing the relationship. The partnership of the two companies generated enough positive momentum in its first twelve months that Elyse was later promoted to Director of Strategic Relationships.

This story illustrates how keeping yourself open to networking opportunities can change your career trajectory for the better, create significant value for your organization, and build lasting strategic relationships.

HOW TO CONNECT AT EVENTS

While the word *networking* is used often, it is an elusive term that people understand differently. Many wonder how to actually network effectively at events. Once you open yourself up to networking, you will be amazed by people's willingness to connect you to people and resources that can help you. The key is to verbalize your interests, needs, or hopes in a way that speaks to people. Once you do, you have a much better chance of getting what you are looking for. Following are some simple strategies that will improve your networking prowess and open up communication.

- **Know how to convey your story**—Have a concise, clear explanation of what you do and where you work. While it is tempting to explain the background of and elaborate on your role, you really need to keep it short and clear. Try to have one general storyline that is worded in laymen's terms, and that you can refine for more technical conversations when speaking with those in your field. Depending on your audience, you will want to convey your role more simply or with more sophisticated language. When in doubt about what your audience knows, go with simple language. You may want to use the "30-second commercial" you created in Chapter 3 to inform your story.

  Example: "Hi, my name is Sarah Willis and I'm a training manager with Haws Mayer. I manage course design, classroom delivery, and in-field coaching for our sales representatives."
- **What did you come to the event to learn?** Articulate what knowledge or experiences you came to the event to acquire.

  Example: "I'm very much looking forward to the preworkshop component of this conference. I am really interested in learning best practices of how trainers can develop their leadership skills."
- **Who did you come to meet?** It is perfectly acceptable to be direct with people about individuals, or profiles of individuals, you would like to meet.

  Example: "I am really hoping to meet and exchange ideas with other professionals in sales training, especially those with several direct reports and that work at large companies like mine."
- **Open-Ended Questioning**—Ask open-ended questions to catalyze networking conversations. This form of dialogue has dual benefits; it

conveys to listeners that you are interested in them and tends to open up discussions. Avoid "yes/no" questions, which usually lead to dead ends.

Examples: "What brought you to this event?" "How did you get into this field?" "What have you learned about our field?" "Where do you see our field moving in the next few years?" "What other kinds of learning/networking events have you found useful?"

- **Your Networking Footprint**—Consider thoughtfully what you want people to remember about you after your conversation. Your final words are a great time to summarize the conversation, particularly if one of you has agreed to help the other in some way.

  Examples: "I really appreciate your offer to introduce me to other sales trainers you meet." "Thanks for agreeing to send me that article on training how-to." "It sounds like we have a lot in common. I would love to stay in touch through LinkedIn."

- **Recap Whom You Met**—At an event where you meet many people, I recommend giving yourself a prompt that will help you distinguish people later. One very easy way to do this is to take the time to write a short note on the back of any business cards you collect. This could be a note about an article you promised to email to a new contact, a snippet of a conversation you had with someone, or even a common thread such as that you both grew up in Philadelphia. Be sure to write important points down; a small note can bring back all the important information you need.

Once you begin using simple networking strategies and keeping yourself open to spontaneous dialogue, you will be amazed at others' willingness to help you. Before you attend an event, try to get clear about what you want and be prepared to thoughtfully articulate it. If you do take the time to clarify what you want, you will get more out of an event because you will more quickly gravitate to your area of need or interest. People cannot help you or connect with you unless you make it known what you want or what you are looking for. The next time you are on your way to an event, ask yourself what you want to get out of it, whom you would like to meet, and what the best-case scenario would be if this event were to serve you well!

THE ART OF FOLLOW-UP

Following up with networking contacts is easier done when you leave your interaction with a clear sense of direction. By concluding interactions with a summary of what your contact can expect next, you are building a bridge to a continued relationship. It is much easier to follow up with someone in a smart, direct way if you have a goal. Do you want to set up a meeting or telephone call with them? Do you want them to become a contact within your LinkedIn circle? If the networking contact gives you advice or additional contacts, follow through on that advice or with the contacts and then update them. I recommend that you notice what method of communication your contact favors and use it when connecting with them. For example, if your contact always emails you back when you leave him or her a voice mail, use email instead. If networking contacts have helped you, think about how you can offer to return the favor. Finally, if a networking contact has been or could be of service to you, a nicely written thank you note goes a long way to foster a positive impression of you and your company.

AUTHENTICITY

Keep in mind that while networking is helped when two people have a certain amount of natural chemistry and likeability, you do not have to become the best of friends to help each other. My best advice here is to put your best foot forward in a networking interaction—be extremely professional and personable, but genuine. If people do not respond to you or like you for who you are, positioning yourself as something you are not will only serve as an anti-strategy.

It can be difficult in networking to differentiate between contrived versus organic relationships. For some, networking has a negative reputation for being an opportunistic practice, self-serving in nature, and often lacking a genuine sense of connection. Barbara A. F. Greene, Chief Executive Officer of Greene and Associates, Inc., remarked, "I don't like the term 'networking,' I prefer 'connecting' instead. Relationships should be lasting and thought of in terms of lifetime relationships, not just an exchange of business cards." Barbara's point is well made and should not be underemphasized. Some good questions to ask yourself before pursuing a contact are listed below to help you distinguish between a truly worthy relationship and one that seems only momentarily beneficial:

- Why do I want to connect with this person?
- What is my intent?
- How do I foresee the two of us interacting?
- What is this person's area of expertise?
- From what I know, do I respect this person?
- How do I want to be like or different from this person?

- What would I like to get from this relationship (information, contacts, experiences had, a door opened, an opinion, to develop my expertise, to collaborate professionally, to sell my product or services, friendship)?
- Do I have expertise or resources that I can share with this person?
- Am I asking for something but not offering anything?
- Am I prepared to articulate what exactly I would like from this person?

As you consider these questions, note that not all networking relationships need to be exactly "50–50." However, if you are the one being helped in a networking relationship and you have not given back to the other person, offers of help can go a long way. Simply stating, "I really appreciate what you've done for me. If there's ever anything I can do for you, please don't hesitate to ask" shows that you want to give back.

FINDING A MENTOR

One of the most invaluable career advancement benefits that networking can yield are mentors. Catherine J. Mathis, Senior Vice President of Corporate Communications at The New York Times Company, shared, "There are many more women to emulate. The fact that progress has been made at the top means that there are more women to observe, women whose behaviors you can mirror, and, of course, more female mentors." I have seen countless situations where mentors, male and female, have helped women to be more successful and move their careers forward. Defined as a trusted advisor, counselor, or guide, mentors are typically experienced people who are willing to help you develop in some way. Mentors act as volunteers, and often have expertise in an area where their mentee wants to develop or improve. Finding a mentor can be as instrumental as networking; however, the two activities have some differences.

Seeking out mentors of both genders that you respect, who handle situations well, and are generally successful will help you. Similar to networking with groups, mentors can give you strategies for traversing organizational obstacles; help uncover your strengths, blind spots, and assumptions; and give you more tools to succeed. Mentor-mentee relationships are a great complement to networking with a group, because they give you private, one-on-one time with your own coach. As you engage mentors, Cathy Fleming suggested, "Be humble, but be direct. . . . Keep in mind that mentors tend to adopt people who look like them, act like them, and think like them. . . . In addition to the invaluable benefit of learning, if you become close to a mentor, you can inherit and share business/clients with him or her, which gives you a big leg up."

Finding a mentor requires that you identify people who have qualities that you admire. These people might also be individuals who have your dream job or position in a company. After you identify whom you would like as a mentor, making a request of their time can be less complex than you think. Katharine Weymouth, Publisher of the *Washington Post* and Chief Executive Officer of Washington Post Media, suggests, "You always want to reach out to people who are smart and successful in their role. Often times they will be willing to give you advice, hear your ideas, and they'll be flattered to be asked. Identify who[m] you admire, who is successful in your company, and just ask, 'Can I get on your calendar?' When younger people approach me this way, I am always impressed." As you engage in your mentoring relationship, try to be a good steward of your mentor's time and energy investment. You can show respect to your mentor by coming prepared, having clear goals, and using their time well.

ASSEMBLING A BOARD OF DIRECTORS

Courteney Monroe, Executive Vice President of Consumer Marketing at HBO, elaborated on the idea of mentors noting, "I think sponsors and mentors can help you, and I see their roles differently. A sponsor looks out for you and advocates for your advancement. I think a mentor is more of a confidante and advisor." Courteney underscores an important point in her remark. You do not need to look to one point-person to satisfy all of your development needs. Reinforcing this point was Naomi C. Earp, Chair of the U.S. Equal Employment Opportunity Commission (EEOC), who advised, "When women look for mentors, they should look for those that will help them grow and stretch, manage their image, and get them exposure. Rarely can you find one person who can help you with all of these, so it is important to seek out mentors to meet each need."

In fact you can approach mentorship as a method for assembling a diverse board of directors for your career. Barbara A. F. Greene encourages women to create their own career advisory boards. She points out, "I guarantee you that if you look at any company with a board, there's usually a lawyer, a real estate person, an accountant and so on. Just as a company surrounds itself with expert coaches, so should a young woman. Surround yourself with people who have skill sets that you don't, and adjust this board of directors as your career goals change." A woman can begin to assemble an advisory board by identifying existing people in her network or organization whom she admires. These advisors are people with important connections and those who want to see you succeed. This board can provide guidance around professional image and presence, expose a mentee to valuable connections, or provide job leads and endorsements.

Just as a code of behavior applies to networking groups, it is also critical to thoughtfully manage the advisor-mentee relationship. Most advisors are more than happy to provide guidance to a protégé who is eager to learn and uses the advisor's time well. Expressing gratitude to advisors is a requirement of the helping relationship. Mentees can also reciprocate their board's generosity by offering to help advisors in their future endeavors. One way that I have tried to repay my mentors, in part, is by writing them glowing recommendations on LinkedIn.

NETWORKS BENEFIT YOUR COMPANY

Your collective network not only can help you as an individual, but also can elevate your organization more than you realize. Dominique Schurman, Chief Executive Officer of Papyrus, told me, "A network of resources that you can go to for different needs is important as an individual, but it also increases your value to a company." While some jobs rely more heavily on your rolodex than others, having a network of different experts makes you much more appealing to a company. In jobs where relationship building is a significant part, such as sales or consulting, your portfolio of contacts becomes even more important.

Some leaders, for example, Roxanne Spillett, President and Chief Executive Officer of Boys and Girls Clubs of America, do not engage in networking for personal benefits as much as for the sake of their organization. Roxanne reflected, "I think [networking] is fine to do if it is in the context of a combination of career strategies. I personally do not network for my own gain; I network to build relationships for the benefit of my organization." At a minimum, networking allows you to promote your company, marketing your products or services. It also helps you strengthen relationships within your community of practice and be perceptive about industry trends.

KEEP CONNECTED

Of all the strategies I discussed with the women I interviewed, effective networking was the single most emphasized recommendation provided for achieving leadership status and career success. As Maya Rockeymoore, Ph.D., President and Founder of Global Policy Solutions, pointed out, "Networking and mentoring are vital. That's probably the number one thing that can help women." Similarly, DeeDee Wilson, Chief Financial Officer at Aritzia, recommended, "I think building a network is the single most important thing younger women can do. I don't mean networking just for the sake of networking; I mean really developing relationships with key decision makers and role models. Networking allows you to gain best practices from others quickly and easily."

Engaging in networking keeps you resilient and up-to-date, and gives you a considerable edge over those that do not network. The investment required of you will likely be far smaller than what you will gain. In my own case, numerous colleagues, classmates, and friends were instrumental in connecting me to resources to write this book. People sent me articles about women leaders, referred candidates to be interviewed for the book, pointed out new gender studies, and many just provided encouragement. I have not forgotten about my network of "helpers," and would gladly go out of my way to connect them with contacts, resources, or jobs in the future. As you broaden your network and see the gains of partaking in it, continually ask yourself how you can be of service to your network. Ultimately, networking is about being genuine and authentic, building trusting, mutually beneficial relationships, and helping others.

SUCCEEDING OFF THE JOB

ACTIVITIES "OFF" THE CLOCK

Since we have examined ways to succeed "on" the job, I would like to shift your attention to activities you can engage in "off" the job that deliver high value. Augmenting work experience with outside activities can bolster a woman's résumé and her confidence. Maximizing time spent off the job can help those who are currently employed, and give direction to women who have stayed at home or otherwise taken a hiatus, and want to transition back into the workforce. This chapter covers the many high-impact initiatives you can undertake with which you will see a return on your time investment. While career advancement is clearly dependent on many forces internal to your workplace, there are many ways that activities outside of work can propel you to new heights.

Supporting this idea is Rosslyn Kleeman, Chair of the Coalition for Effective Change, who said, "It's crucial to engage in activities outside of work for professional growth and because it gives you something personally. Any activities you can engage in that broaden you as a person will make you smarter, more interesting and more likely to move up at work." Like Rosslyn, many women I interviewed strongly encouraged young women to develop themselves inside and outside of the office. They also recommended strategies to bolster one's work portfolio in ways that satisfy your most closely held values.

Those women I interviewed verbalized a noteworthy qualification with regard to engaging in outside activities; many warned that you should only engage in such activities if your on-the-job performance is solid and well regarded. Illustrating this point, Shannon S. S. Herzfeld, Vice President of Government Relations at Archer Daniels Midland Company, recommended, "[D]on't pursue activities outside of work unless you are performing on the job at an A+ level." Denise Incandela, President of Saks Direct at Saks Fifth Avenue, echoed this sentiment advising, "Be careful not to over extend yourself. You don't want to take on outside roles if you're not already doing a great job in the office." If you engage in too many outside activities prematurely in a job or when you are not performing well, these outside activities can serve to distract you more than anything from your daily work performance.

KNOW YOUR INDUSTRY

One very concrete strategy for bolstering your contribution to an organization is to become more knowledgeable about your industry as a whole. Regardless if you are junior or high ranking, having an informed view of your industry will make you smarter and more valuable to your organization. Courteney Monroe, Executive Vice President of Consumer Marketing at HBO, suggests, "Read everything you can on your field and your company. In my case, I need to be an avid consumer of entertainment . . . I also make a point to see what our competitors are doing." Having an understanding of your industry can help you make better decisions that reflect the broader environment you work in.

Additionally, staying informed of industry trends will demonstrate that you see outside of your organization's walls. A smart place to begin investing your energy, therefore, is to familiarize yourself with your industry's vulnerabilities, strengths, and the market forces that affect it. Many professionals overlook studying their own industry, and over-focus instead only on the daily job they do or the company in which they work. Warning against this approach, Alexandra Miller, Chief Executive Officer of Mercedes Medical, Inc., recommended, "Read industry journals, attend trade shows, join industry groups. I'm amazed at the amount of people that don't read up on their own fields. Knowledge is power and the sooner young women learn that the better."

Being educated on developments in your field can quickly increase your chances of having an intelligent angle to share or bringing a needed insight to a meeting. By reading publications, for example, you can stay well connected to helpful resources and breaking industry news. Examples of relevant publications depend on your industry and functional role; however, business books and journals, newspapers, magazines, periodicals, blogs, and Web sites that pertain in some way to your work are good examples. Consider researching these publications in addition to subscribing to applicable newsletters. See if your company will pay for your membership in industry network associations; often associations put out magazines or articles for distribution, many of which are free if you are already a member.

The key to staying afloat in a "knowledge economy" like ours is to adopt the task of staying current on your field as one of your main job responsibilities. Donna Callejon, Chief Operating Officer at GlobalGiving, provides an additional insight, noting, "Find out what your boss reads, and stay current on it so that you can discuss the same trends and news." Reading the same publications as your boss sends the message that you prioritize learning relevant news, that the two of you are more alike than dissimilar, and, subsequently, that you also are future management material.

Staying current also gives you material for an underestimated use—professional small talk. Carla E. Lucchino, Assistant Deputy Commandant, Installations and Logistics at the U.S. Marine Corps, mentioned this advantage, noting, "I think staying current by reading often is helpful. I'd suggest reading newspapers so that you can be conversant and make small talk, which I need to do often." Personally, I have also found that in consulting, for example, rapport-building with clients is such a critical part of the consulting engagement that often the most substantive work does not begin until a solid rapport is first established. Being able to weave industry and on-the-job knowledge into these conversations helps increase your credibility and show that you can be trusted as the project progresses and unfolds.

Similarly, when I asked Cynthia Egan, President of Retirement Plan Services at T. Rowe Price, what competencies or skills made her most promotable, she cited, "Making it my business to know my business." Whether or not it is in your job description, understanding what outlets are available for industry information and using them to stay informed is a basic requirement of an aspiring leader. For example, a financial analyst working for an insurance company may want to consult a cross-section of publications—ranging from publications such as the *Wall Street Journal* and the *Financial Times,* to a Financial Analysts blog, and perhaps even a niche publication from a financial women's association or based on the insurance industry. Providing yet another idea, Catherine J. Mathis, Senior Vice President of Corporate Communications at The New York Times Company, suggests reading transcripts of speeches. Reading a variety of publications is guaranteed to help broaden your knowledge. As you find new outlets for knowledge, be creative in what information you seek out.

THE COMPETITIVE LANDSCAPE

Can you easily answer the question, "Who are your organization's competitors?" You should not only be able to respond knowledgeably to that question, but also be able to say a few words about each of your competitors' approaches. Regardless of whom your organization serves, and whether you work for a for-profit or nonprofit organization, I guarantee that competitors exist who are seeking the same customers, vendors, clients, or donors as you. When I asked D'Arcy Foster Rudnay, Senior Vice President for Comcast Corporation, what strategy for advancing one's career goes overlooked most, she noted, "Young people don't always look beyond their own job—or the company they work for—to understand the big picture. It's not enough to keep up with what your company is doing, you need to also read competitor data and really understand the broader business environment."

Many of your competitors' company Web sites can give you useful data—from how they brand and position their products or services to who their central client, consumer, or audience base is. Catherine J. Mathis shares, "Read about your competitors and be knowledgeable about what they offer their customers, their competitive position, their financials." Many company Web sites allow you to consult annual reviews, brochures, press releases, proxy statements, executive biographies, and 10-Ks. I personally find 10-Ks to be the most valuable document to consult of those listed if the company you are studying is publicly traded.

As part of your research on competitors, you may want to research what kinds of tools they use, both with customers and internally. In-person networking is a valuable way to learn about such practices, since many companies do not post this information freely on their Web sites. You might ask a networking acquaintance an open-ended question such as, "How does your firm handle the task of customer relationship management?" Such a question might yield good information containing anything from how the company staffs their customer relationship management function internally, to what brand of tools they have used, to what they plan to do about customer relationship management in the future.

Building on this idea, consider researching tools and efficiency systems that streamline the day-to-day work of your competitors. Dominique Schurman, Chief Executive Officer of Papyrus, specifically advised, "The more skills you have, the better. There are proven management systems, methods and tools that exist which can really make a difference in efficiency. . . . An example of one such tool is a decision log. My company uses this document to designate action items and action 'owners' following each meeting. This may sound simple, but it's a powerful way to build consensus and streamline communication." Whatever you can learn from your competitors, whether from their project failures or their major successes, use their experiences and information to bring new practices to your workplace.

IN-PERSON NETWORKING

In-person networking events are also an excellent way to stay informed. Networking is so critical, in fact, to staying informed that I designated an entire chapter—Chapter 4—of this book to it. Here, I will cover only a few key elements of networking. Networking events can build alliances that may serve you and your business in the future, keep you informed of competitors in your industry, and, most of all, give you access to trends and strategies that you can apply to your own company. Catherine J. Mathis shared, "I find that collaborating with colleagues internally and externally is very useful. I am on the Board of the National Investor Relations Institute (NIRI) where I have the opportunity to interact with communications professionals, leaders, writers, and thinkers. . . . Networking gives you a better understanding of what's going on in your industry and what ideas might be helpful in your business."

CONFERENCES AND WEBINARS

Conferences and other in-person learning events can certainly serve to add to your knowledge bank. Courteney Monroe suggests, "Go to conferences and tradeshows and really try to immerse yourself in what your company does." Webinars provide yet another, highly interactive and convenient medium for learning and development. By engaging in conferences and webinars you can hear firsthand about current research, experimentation, and best practices of your industry group. Many such events encourage participation and discussion, which can spur useful thinking and ideas that you can bring back to the office. Further, conferences, in particular, can have the effect of reenergizing us when we are feeling burned-out or uninspired.

JOINING ASSOCIATIONS

Another way to stay well networked and informed is to join industry or other associations. Why bother engaging in associations? Broadening your network of contacts will help not only you as an individual but also your organization to prosper. You will contribute to your organization by having a rolodex that your organization can leverage. Dominique Schurman reflected, "Professional organizations can help you to stay current on your industry. The reality is that you get caught up in your work and outside activities can be tough to accommodate time-wise. Nonetheless, you can add value to your organization. . . ." Regardless of the time commitments involved, carefully chosen networking activities can often return more value than energy invested.

Joining associations and groups may also prove useful when your competencies are either minimized or altogether invisible to your current employer. Maya Rockeymoore, Ph.D., President and Founder of Global Policy Solutions, shares, "Sometimes when your strengths are overlooked within your immediate organization, you need outsiders to affirm your talents. This is especially important from a networking perspective, because often times your employer will respect you more when they see that other outside groups respect you." Using networking groups and associations as a career safety net is a wise move, particularly in our current economic climate. Furthermore, if you get a confidence boost from being a valued member of an association or networking group, all the better! Participation as a member of an association, and even more so as a representative of an association, tells your employer you are ambitious and want more from life than just staying in your current role.

COMPANY EVENTS

Attending events hosted by your employer, whether happy hours, company picnics, or holiday parties, can be a good way to stay informed, socially and professionally. Shannon S. S. Herzfeld encouraged, "Events outside of work provide access to more networking opportunities. Go to that company softball game or happy hour." Attending such events can help you learn about how others have traversed obstacles at the company, whether those obstacles involve difficult people or situations.

A SUBSTANTIVE VOLUNTEER ROLE

One of the biggest ways to augment your credentials is to get involved formally with a nonprofit organization. In the best-case scenario, you can participate in the work of a nonprofit that has some kind of tie to your organization. When first joining associations, I suggest you simply take on a membership role in which you can absorb how the organization functions and what it really stands for. If you perceive a match in your values and the values of the organization, however, I would advise looking for substantive volunteer positions with a leadership component. Examples of leadership opportunities include handling the finances of a fundraiser, managing an annual event from start to finish, or serving on the search committee for a new board member.

Whatever the volunteer challenge, look for opportunities to manage or lead people or processes. Doing so can give you invaluable experience, which can sometimes propel you into leadership positions both with your volunteer organization and with your full-time employer. Maya Rockeymoore advises, "Volunteering at a non profit or for a political campaign often comes with significant responsibility and can help bolster a young woman's résumé. There are many transferable skills that you can cite on your résumé."

Shannon S. S. Herzfeld expressed a similar idea: "Consider volunteering in a philanthropic capacity that is a 'two-fer.' That is, make sure the opportunity is both of interest to you and is also contributing to some greater good." The ideal volunteering positions feed you personally and ultimately make your contribution to the organization even stronger. Agreeing with this point is Cathy Fleming, Partner at Nixon Peabody LLP, who said, "Assuming you already have a degree, any involvement in an organization can help, whether it's working in your children's school or being on the board of a non-profit. . . . You should always pick an activity for which you have a passion. Activities help you network with new people, meet people from different backgrounds, and make you a happier, more fulfilled person." Notice that the advice provided here is not to join associations or take on roles solely as a means to build your résumé. The best opportunities are ones where you have a natural connection to the organization or initiative and its mission.

You may receive offers to do menial work in the nonprofit organizations you join. If that satisfies you—by all means do it—but know that it will not really build your professional credentials. Kelly Pickett, a senior manager at a management consulting firm, put it best when she suggested, "Volunteer early in your career—and I don't mean the kind of volunteering where you run a drink stand. Take a substantive role in an organization, like accounting, planning or structuring an event. You can get significant skill and management development from that kind of experience. I personally prefer a smaller organization where I can have a more hands-on opportunity to learn." Many small, and consequently short-staffed, organizations will appreciate any added time, help, or expertise they can get. Review the following steps as you think about where and how you could pursue a volunteer role:

Volunteer Strategies

1. Identify a passion or interest of importance to you.
2. Look for causes and organizations whose work matches your passions and interests.
3. Consider what skills you can contribute and what kind of roles you are most interested in serving.
4. Identify new skills you would like to learn.
5. Outline the kind of time commitment you are able and are willing to make.

6. Look for "win-win-win" volunteer opportunities that could satisfy you, the organization you will serve, and your employer.
7. Demonstrate the results of your volunteer work, preferably quantifiably.
8. Translate your volunteer work and results to your full-time job.

A BOARD ROLE

A role on a nonprofit organization's board can be a formal way to recognize your contribution. Board roles also carry a certain weight that other volunteer opportunities do not. Generally speaking, the role of a board is to provide oversight and support to an organization's chief executive. This leadership group is responsible for ensuring that the organization meets its mission and goals, and has support and a favorable standing within the community.

DeeDee Wilson, Chief Financial Officer at Aritzia, recommended, "Get involved in the board of a non-profit organization. This will allow you to learn leadership skills in a smaller, safer environment." Similarly, Patricia Deyton, Director of the Center for Gender in Organizations at Simmons School of Management, advised, "Look for a governance role or a board role. Often times, small non-profits are willing to have less experienced people on their boards." So why would a nonprofit organization want a board member who has less than executive experience? Quite simply— need. Many nonprofit organizations survive with remarkably few human and tangible resources. If you have assistance to offer, make a good case as to why and how you can make a contribution that will help the organization.

Board roles can carry significant responsibility since they represent one of the highest-ranking positions of a nonprofit organization. The transferable skills available to you after taking a board role are therefore numerous. Cuc T. Vu, Chief Diversity Officer at Human Rights Campaign, advised, "You can find deep meaning by having an active civic life. Think outside of your full-time role. You can get catapulted into leadership positions in non profits and end up as a co-chair or doing radio spots or interviews for the organization." Know that as you progress through your career, your involvement in different organizations can change along with your interests and passions. Jeanine Becker, Senior Counsel at Motorola, Inc., recalled, "I've volunteered on a few non-profit boards, looking specifically for those that fuel my passion and excite me. For me, I'm particularly interested in women's rights and advocacy. I spent years working for those causes, but when I turned to corporate work full time, I never lost the original piece of me that was passionate about those issues. So I found different ways over time to grow and expand my skills and at the same time stay connected to my passions."

Many resources exist to connect nonprofit organizations with volunteers. Some even exist to connect nonprofit organizations to people interested in board opportunities. Examples of well-established online resources include:

- www.networkforgood.org
- www.volunteermatch.org
- www.SmartVolunteer.org
- www.VillageVolunteers.org
- www.boardnetusa.org
- www.boardconnect.org
- www.businessvolunteers.org/board.htm

TRANSFERRING YOUR VOLUNTEERING EXPERIENCE TO THE JOB

To get the most out of volunteering, make sure you can demonstrate that you achieved results. Just as you would with other jobs on your résumé, look for ways to quantify your achievements using financial data or other metrics. Tell a compelling story about what you did for the non-profit organization and why you did it. Once you have an interesting and persuasive explanation, use this experience to advocate for other high-level assignments at your job. Erin McGinnis, National Committee Chair of the Society of Women Engineers, takes this notion a step further, advising, "I'm part of the Society of Women Engineers and the Society of Manufacturing Engineers. I work hard to find opportunities to lead people and/or manage projects within these groups. Then if a boss questions my ability to take on new responsibilities, I can say 'Look what I've taken part in and the kind of role I've played.' I've found lots of benefits from these outside activities." Roles you play outside of your job can serve to substantiate your skill base and capabilities.

While Cathy Fleming has had a highly impressive career where she has held many leadership roles, she reported, "I'm most proud that I was asked to be the President of the National Association of Women Lawyers (NAWL). That was the highlight of my career. I have enormous respect for the attorneys in that group—they are the cream of the crop in terms of smart, capable women. It was a truly humbling experience." If you feel hungry to take on new risks or feel stifled in your current job role, think big by considering where else you could channel your drive and energy. Do not place limits on yourself, but instead follow your interests and passions and keep yourself open to possibilities. As Rosslyn Kleeman recommends of those considering volunteer work, "Don't just put your name on a list, do something substantive."

"SECOND" JOBS

Jobs outside of your full-time work can also carry solid, transferable experience in relation to your day job. I recommend that you use skills from outside jobs to build your confidence and test new skills. Patricia Deyton indicated, "I tell the undergraduate students I teach that even if they manage a shift at a restaurant, they are still managing complexities and getting valuable experience. I also tell them that management makes the world go 'round. When you manage, you need to be able to articulate your skills and show results." While experience gained as a waitress, for example, may not be compelling to a business employer, I suggest using such second jobs to build your confidence and experiment with your skills. As a waitress, you might learn that you have a high tolerance for stress, that you can serve ten tables at once and still remain calm and competent. That kind of insight into yourself will have a positive effect on your day job as well. The skills of multitasking and managing multiple priorities are required in almost every job; let an experience like this help convince you even more of your abilities!

Look around at the myriad of places in your life where you are spearheading projects or coordinating resources. Karen Holbrook, Ph.D., Vice President of Research and Innovation at University of South Florida and immediate past president of Ohio State University, urged, "Don't undervalue your experiences. Many overlook and underestimate the types of experiences they have had or projects they have managed."

LEVERAGE YOUR EDUCATION

Your education is an important aspect of your overall professional profile. Clearly, education is something that you can pursue "off the job" that can distinguish you competitively. Pursuing education is also one of the most effective things you can do to personally grow and evolve. Furthermore, your educational network, including professors and classmates, can be called upon throughout your life as a useful part of your larger network. When it comes to holding a top position at an organization, a solid education can be one more distinguishing factor that sets you apart from other candidates and gives you an edge.

The very best training opportunities for aspiring leaders are ones that give you something personally and professionally, and provide you with an analytical, problem-solving knowledge base. Many different disciplines can teach such skills, so it is up to you to find an academic outlet that best suits your interests and needs. Remembering her own academic experience, Jamie McCourt, President of the Los Angeles Dodgers, shared, "I've received a lot of training that helped me in the end game. I practiced law—even though it was not my true calling—and my legal training and law degree have proven to be invaluable tools. My legal background trained me to see problems, analyze them, and look for solutions. There is a rigor in law school that changes how you think and problem-solve, and it translates well to business."

Several of the women I interviewed either credited an MBA as having helped them or cited that they wished they had pursued an MBA for the financial and business acumen it provides. One such comment came from Autumn Bayles, Senior Vice President of Strategic Operations at Tasty Baking Company, who noted, "The more training you have, the better. An MBA is especially nice because it gives you a broad background and is universally accepted as credible." Autumn went on to say, "Having an MBA, especially from Wharton or any other well known school, can really open doors. I think it's also helped me to have an engineering background because it's trained me to think in a very analytical way."

On the topic of business education, Jeanine Becker noted, "I wish I had gotten a JD and an MBA. At the time I went to law school, I wasn't thinking about the power of business for social change. Where my legal training focused on assessing and limiting risk, business teaches you to have a healthy tolerance for risk. Whether you get that mindset from school or your own life experience, I've learned that over the course of my life, most important decisions are made with imperfect information—and that a business mindset helps to see the risk, mitigate it and make conscious choices to move forward." Katharine Weymouth, Publisher of the *Washington Post* and Chief Executive Officer of Washington Post Media, was yet another person I interviewed who mentioned the value of an MBA. She related, "I wish I'd done an MBA early on because I deal with business on a daily basis and could use the financial training."

Even though education can give women tremendous confidence, you often need a certain measure of confidence just to apply to be in a program. This can hold some women back from continuing their education at all. An example is Barbara A. F. Greene, Chief Executive Officer of Greene and Associates, Inc., who shared, "I might have gone for an MBA but I never saw myself in business. I lacked confidence, even though I ended up a business owner. This is another reason why you need your own personal board of directors to show that they believe in you and give you that confidence." Building on this sentiment, when I asked Lora J. Villarreal, Ph.D., Executive Vice President and Chief People Officer at Affiliated Computer Services, Inc. (ACS), what she wished she had known at the beginning of her career, she reflected, "To be more confident. Before I received my education (my master's and doctoral degrees), I thought everyone was smarter than me. I was wrong. I had what I needed but I lacked the self-esteem and confidence at the time. Today, I realize there are no limits to what an individual can achieve." Do not let your confidence get the best of you when considering augmenting your education. While you may have to take a leap of faith, the results will be worth it. Jeanine Becker underscored the importance of first-hand experience when she encouraged, "Get out there and try things, do an internship, take a class . . . "

ADDITIONAL DEGREES

Adding to your current credentials by pursuing continuing education, whether through succinct training experiences or a more prolonged degree, is a step that can vastly improve your credibility, competitiveness, and market value. The key finding from my research in this area was simple: Young women are encouraged to obtain as much training as they can, and seek out an advanced degree from the best school they can possibly afford. Business and law degrees were credited most as giving the women I interviewed the most analytical rigor they needed as leaders. Cathy Fleming candidly noted, "[I]t helped that I attended an excellent women's college and an Ivy League law school. My classmates were smart, terrific colleagues; many are still my friends." Naomi C. Earp, Chair of the U.S. Equal Employment Opportunity Commission (EEOC), also noted, "Having a law degree has made me more marketable—and law is almost the perfect complement to any previous training a person has. I started out studying social work but a law degree certainly made me more bankable."

Educational credentials also help people, particularly young people, get more respect. When I asked Rosslyn Kleeman what traits or habits helped her to be taken seriously at work, she shared, "Being well-educated. Keep learning and always take advantage of training opportunities. A woman, especially a young woman, is given more respect if she's educated." Katharine Weymouth also suggested that advanced education plays a role in getting credibility and respect. She noted, "Having an advanced, second degree like a JD, MBA or other Masters degree really helps in being taken seriously."

TRAINING TOPICS

If pursuing an advanced degree does not meet your needs, there is also considerable value to be had in less formal training. Mei Xu, Founder and Chief Executive Officer of Chesapeake Bay Candle, Blissliving Home, discussed how the economy has affected companies' willingness to fund professional development, noting, "Training is under siege right now for a lot of companies.... If you do pursue formal training, make sure it is specific and relevant to your chosen field. Whatever training you attend, make sure you can measure the results of it."

If you want to get training and experience without pursuing a degree, many of the women I interviewed recommended certain training topics. The most often mentioned topics include leadership, negotiation, communication, and business development skills. The other point many women made was that young women need to address those areas in which they know they are weak or where they need more knowledge to do a great job.

Reinforcing this point was Carla E. Lucchino. Carla recommended, "Don't just go after training that you're already expert in, seek out opportunities that broaden your expertise." She went on to say, "Leadership training is important because some women are easily intimidated and don't know how to handle it. Others don't necessarily see themselves as leaders and need training to have a strong presence. When I was overseas doing work in Saudi Arabia, I'd ask a man a question and he would only give an answer—and his eye contact—to my male colleagues. You have to be able to manage that kind of situation and deal with it even if you don't like it."

Erin McGinnis takes this notion a step further, advising, "If you struggle to maintain who you are as a woman in a male-driven industry, there are programs like UCLA Extension for women leaders. Sometimes in engineering, women can take on a totally male leadership style, and women's programs like UCLA's can help you find an integrated male and female voice."

Leadership training is useful for understanding the role of an effective leader and assessing your own natural leadership style. Melissa M. Monk, Chief Infrastructure Officer at Capital One, noted, "I would recommend training in leadership, since women have a tendency to want to people-please. Areas that are especially important are learning to influence, having a presence, and becoming an inspirational leader. A lot of good companies will help you develop these skills. During my seven years at Capital One, I've probably taken over 50 classes from statistics modeling, to leadership presence, to influence, and executive leadership in the community." Training focused on leadership can also be helpful in identifying how to involve team members to a lesser or greater degree, depending on the circumstances of the situation.

While many of us are more inclined to augment our technical skills in favor of our "softer" skills, increasingly research tells us that it is soft skills training that is most lacking. A 2008 study conducted by the Graduate Management Admission Council (GMAC), for example, surveyed MBA graduates to understand how their degrees served them on the job. When asked what knowledge and skills they wish they had acquired (or acquired to a greater extent) as part of their MBA education, soft skills rose to the surface. In retrospect, MBA alumni say they wish they had received more education or training in the following areas:

- Managing human capital
- Managing the decision-making process
- Managing strategy and innovation
- Interpersonal skills
- Strategic and system skills (GMAC, 2008)

Clearly, there is value to be had in sharpening your leadership skills. Cynthia Egan presented yet another strategy for learning, citing, "Identify one or two areas where you really want to develop and go after those. There is important learning to be had during the process of seeking certifications and licenses. Do what you can to practice communication and public speaking skills."

Trainings can be provided in-house by your employer, through universities' and colleges' continuing education programs, or through companies that specialize in training for working professionals. Certainly, some training comes with a certificate or certification designation, which is that much better since it will bolster your résumé and credentials. I encourage you to negotiate with your employer to understand what, if any, training funds can be provided by your employer. If there is no policy on tuition reimbursement or training funding, negotiate with your employer about how a given training will bring the organization value. This is an area where women tend to under-negotiate, perhaps because they are afraid to "put their employer out." Do not be seduced by being accommodating. Remember, ask for what you want!

YOUR EDUCATIONAL NETWORK

As a final word on continuing your education, think about leveraging your school contacts throughout your future. Obviously, to do this, you need to stay in touch with key contacts. Jeanine Becker shared how she manages this process, noting, "Since I left law school, all the jobs I've gotten have materialized from people I know. I did small things to foster my relationships, like send e-cards at the holidays. While not as personal as a handwritten card, they are much easier for someone to reply to and continue the dialogue. In fact, my current position at Motorola came when I sent such an e-card and my current manager responded with a request for a résumé." There are small things you can do, just as you would within your network, to nurture relationships. Consider how you can be of service to your classmates and professors and how they can help you.

INTERNSHIPS/FELLOWSHIPS

One other concrete activity you can pursue off the job to gain experience, is to take an internship or apprenticeship somewhere. Maya Rockeymoore recommends, "Get a wide variety of experiences so that you can really live up to your potential. Varied experiences provide women with an opportunity to see what they are good at and to strengthen their talents and assets. Fellowships and internships are formal ways to dip your foot into certain fields to see if they're right for you." Use internship opportunities to broaden yourself and observe what intrigues you and what does not. Universities are great places to locate internships since they have so many strategic alliances already in place with businesses. If there are no alliances in place with the organization you are interested in, ask the university if you can form one and blaze a new trail. If all else fails, approach the organization yourself and request an informational interview.

SELF-DEVELOPMENT

When I asked Naomi C. Earp what outside activities help supplement a woman's portfolio, she offered, "Become a community member. . . . You can also get involved in faith-based groups through a church or synagogue. These kind of commitments can be time-consuming at first but they're worth it." Do not limit yourself and your leadership abilities to industry associations alone. There are plenty of leadership opportunities, in all kinds of forums and groups, just waiting to be claimed and managed.

There are also many aspects of self-development that can help you on the job. The more aware you are of both your strengths and opportunities for improvement, the more you can leverage your gifts and strengthen your weak points. Additionally, the more authentic and whole you are as a person, the less you will feel you have to wear a mask at work. Cuc T. Vu told me about her experience in this area. She advised, "Read *The 8th Habit* by Stephen Covey. Find your voice. You'll be surprised by what you have to say when you actually hear yourself out loud and don't just think things privately." She went on to say, "Being authentic is important. You can't build trust if you don't show your true self. For me, being 'out' as a gay woman with immigrant roots is an important part of bringing my whole self to work."

What are some ways that you can develop yourself? How can you foster more authenticity? Outside of being your authentic, whole self, what other activities can you partake in that broaden and diversify you? Some activities that can help you stay buoyant and develop personally include:

- **Feed Your Aspirations**—Read biographies or take in other inspirational media about people whom you aspire to be like.
- **Be Mindful**—Being mindful is about focusing on your effects on others, being present and living in the now, and letting go of what you cannot control.
- **Affirmation**—Reading affirmative books and literature or engaging in your own self-affirming exercises, such as journaling, are wonderful ways to be reflective and boost your confidence.
- **Fun**—Good, old-fashioned fun—the kind that makes you laugh and feel joyful—is a great way to nurture yourself. Most of all, it helps you take things more lightly, get needed perspective, and let go of stress.
- **Relaxation**—Whether through body massage, breathing work, meditation, or practices such as yoga, look for activities that relax and center you.
- **Hobbies**—Investing in activities that feed your passion and interest will only serve to nourish you personally and make you a more interesting, well-rounded person at work. Whether it is gourmet cooking, scrapbooking, or writing, give it your energy and you will see gains in professional areas of your life as well.

SPORTS-RELATED GROWTH OPPORTUNITIES

Sports and fitness is yet another activity you can engage in off the job that can build your confidence and reduce stress. Roxanne Spillett, President and Chief Executive Officer of Boys and Girls Clubs of America, cited even more benefits of exercise, noting, "I think sports and fitness are a great way to keep your mind and body active. Whether you participate in sports or enjoy them as an observer, they give you a better eye for strategy, competition, and help you strike up conversations with work contacts—especially men." Furthermore, significant research substantiates a positive relationship between higher levels of exercise activity and higher levels of self-esteem. In a study of male and female elementary school, high school, and university students, for example, a consistent finding was that exercise had a beneficial effect on how participants felt about themselves (Frost & McKelvie, 2005). Exercise is beneficial from many angles and can empower women leaders in the making by showing them that they have grit, tenacity, and perseverance—all traits needed to run a company.

You can also look for leadership opportunities within the sports and fitness realm. Denise Incandela advised, "Any leadership roles are good activities. It doesn't have to be work-related. You can work with a charity or join a running league—anything that gives you experience leading others."

Exercise can help you gain a level of comfort with your body that helps you embrace and own your physicality. Why is "body comfort" important at work? The leadership presence and confidence you project in a boardroom comes in part from how you feel about your body. Exercise can also have the effect of clearing your mind and giving you a clean mental slate. A compelling case can be made for engaging in or leading others in physical activity; it benefits you physically, mentally, emotionally, and intellectually.

BROADEN YOUR CULTURAL COMPETENCE

Yet another overlooked strategy for making oneself more competitive is to develop culture competence. In today's "flat" global economy, cultural awareness and competence are necessary and marketable skills. More than any generation before us, there is an emphasis on global collaboration, outsourcing, and decentralized companies, a trend which is only growing.

You can develop your cultural competence in many ways—through travel, by learning new languages, educating yourself about different cultures, or taking international work assignments. Certainly the business case for an inclusive and diverse approach has already been made persuasively. Living a life that allows you to be a part of diverse experiences, by meeting people who are different from you, for instance, will always serve to expand your thinking and open your mind. A frequently mentioned interview topic, Mei Xu advised, "You really have to diversify yourself. Even in your personal life, go out and enjoy a taco or dumpling with someone from another culture. If you don't come from a diverse family or community, get educated by interacting with international students. Go to their restaurants and mingle with their circle of friends. You will become enriched and learn new ways of communicating and resolving issues. You will also find that you give people the benefit of the doubt more often."

Looking back at her experience of cultural learning, Cuc T. Vu advised, "For me, much of my journey and learning has been cultural. In Asian culture, often the person who speaks least is seen as the smartest. In American culture, the person who speaks most often is seen as the smartest. I didn't know that when I first started out." Exposing yourself to different facets of global culture is a great way to make you more adaptable, knowledgeable, and able to think strategically.

Experiencing foreign travel can certainly provide you with a fulfilling experience personally and professionally. Catherine J. Mathis commented, "Experiences like traveling, which I love to do, help me to see business more broadly. Not only is it intellectually stimulating, but makes the things I read about come alive. It has given me a deeper appreciation of how the press works. I have found that traveling experiences have been useful in many work situations, particularly in understanding how foreign governments function." Clearly, the experience of travel can serve you on many levels.

MAKE YOURSELF MORE COMPETITIVE

Have you received awards, scholarships, or honors? If so, do you promote them on your biography or résumé? I encourage you to distinguish yourself by leveraging accolades you have received. If you have already received such awards, make sure they are part of your résumé and your professional profile on social networking sites. Consider also applying for additional honors and awards, including scholarships, internal company awards, and regional prizes. Some ways to do this are in the forms of school-based competitions, scholarships, and distinguished persons registries. You can also look for regional or local competitions, such as many business journals' "Forty Under 40" lists, in which 40 people under the age of 40 are honored for their achievements. Promote your achievements and look for new opportunities to get recognition for your excellent work.

OUTSIDE ACTIVITIES CAN MAKE ALL THE DIFFERENCE

Differentiating yourself means being able to offer your employer a broad range of needed competencies. To that end, D'Arcy Foster Rudnay shared, "You always want to position and package yourself as having many different skills." There is simply no better way to do that than by diversifying the kinds of activities you engage in. As you think big, consider creatively how off-the-job activities can help pave a path to your leadership goals. Jeanine Becker advised, "My position as a lecturer teaching negotiation at Stanford Law School took 10 months to come to fruition. I didn't give up. I had to keep pushing and building the relationships . . . and waiting. . . . Don't take 'no' for an answer and *practice* patience."

Negotiating for What You Want

THE ART OF ASKING

The women I interviewed noted that negotiation is an absolutely critical element of moving a career forward. If you think about it, women negotiate with many different people and in many day-to-day ways, often without even realizing they are in a bargaining situation. Whether the negotiation is a small, everyday matter, or a bigger, more structured deal, making the most of these conversations is important. Negotiation, of course, is a complex art given the fact that its subjects are human beings, with distinct thoughts, ideas, and experiences that they bring to the experience. Practice, as well as formalized training, can improve a woman's negotiation skill set immeasurably. Naomi C. Earp, Chair of the U.S. Equal Employment Opportunity Commission (EEOC), expands this idea, commenting, "All women should take at least one course on negotiation for personal and professional reasons. This can help give you the skills to ask for a raise or bonus from your boss, or even negotiate effectively with a car mechanic."

FORMS OF NEGOTIATION

Negotiation can occur in obvious ways as well as many subtler ways. Some of the more traditional matters that we negotiate include job offers, closing deals at work, or making a case or argument for something. Jeanine Becker, Senior Counsel at Motorola, Inc., points out some of the more nuanced ways women negotiate, citing, "Women are juggling many things and in the process we are also negotiating all the time, from what movie to see with friends, to getting your child to eat one more bite of vegetables, to what work assignments we take on. Think about the times you've negotiated successfully and gain confidence from those experiences, and also recognize that negotiation is a skill set that we can practice and improve." Unfortunately, for many women, much of negotiation is halted before the bargaining conversation even begins. So many women overlook negotiating altogether!

You can use negotiation for many things. Many negotiate to get something they want, keep something they have, or move through a conflict. Others negotiate to strengthen a relationship. You can use negotiation techniques with colleagues, employees, your manager, vendors, customers, and in your personal relationships. You can also use the skills of negotiating when you are unsatisfied with a product, service, or experience.

RESEARCH ON WOMEN AND NEGOTIATION

Linda Babcock and Sara Laschever (2003) have done some truly invaluable research on gender and negotiations. Their landmark book, *Women Don't Ask: Negotiation and the Gender Divide,* which I strongly suggest that you read, provides powerful insight into women and negotiation. While serving as a director at Carnegie Mellon's Heinz School of Public Policy and Management Ph.D. program, Babcock noticed distinct differences in the nature and frequency of the requests her male and female students made. In collaboration with colleagues, Babcock conducted numerous studies, which showed that women are much less likely than men to use negotiation or to ask for what they want. Her well-articulated book makes the argument that women need to negotiate more than ever on their own behalf. After all, women are leaving the home more, changing jobs more often, and going through other experiences that often require negotiation skills, such as divorce, home-buying, and starting businesses.

Why is negotiating so difficult to women? For one thing, Babcock and Laschever's surveys point to a negative association with negotiation, showing that women report feeling "a great deal of apprehension" about negotiation—at a rate 2.5 times more than men (2003). Another interesting finding, when asked to pick metaphors that represent the practice of negotiating, women selected "going to the dentist" while men more often selected "winning a ballgame" and "a wrestling match." If you consider the differences in opinion for a moment, isn't it interesting that women equate the event of negotiation to something as passive as a dentist appointment—something that is being done to them—while men see themselves as an active participant in a strategic sporting match?

Babcock's research also shows that women have a less optimistic view of the possible outcomes of their negotiations, creating a dynamic where they ask for less, on average, 30 percent less than men do (Babcock & Laschever, 2003). A key reason behind women under-positioning themselves may be related to a desire to preserve relationships. Women put such a significant focus on forming and maintaining relationships—a trait that helps them in many ways in business, but can handicap them in negotiations. Certainly, relationships are critical in the workplace. A woman needs to weigh, however, if and when the relationship is more important than the outcome of the negotiation.

Negotiation and confrontation are often seen as interrelated. Courtney Monroe, Executive Vice President of Consumer Marketing at HBO, urges women to get more comfortable with direct exchanges, noting, "I think women could use more training in confrontation and tough conversations. I see a need to be liked in myself and other women. Relationships are great, but you have to be able to embrace confrontation." Clearly women do not lack aspirations and ambition. Rather many value the relationships they have formed; in some cases, more than they value their own desires and personal agenda.

GOOD WORK DOES NOT GUARANTEE REWARDS

Numerous interviews I conducted pointed to a belief that many young women have mistakenly "swallowed whole." Naomi C. Earp summarized this idea when she said, "There's an expectation that the 'system' will recognize and reward us when we do good work." Many of us have been conditioned to believe that if we keep our heads down and produce good results, we will consequently be promoted or recognized in some way. Earp went on to say, "It's not true—it's up to us to negotiate promotions, raises, bonuses and respectfully disagree with our boss if we're turned down." While this concept can be disheartening at first, once you shift your thinking around it, you will be able to move past any injustice and act on your own behalf fully. Realize that if you are not being rewarded or recognized fairly, you need to speak up and ask for what you want.

Jamie McCourt, President of the Los Angeles Dodgers, added further insight around this issue, sharing, "In my experience as an employer and an employee, women don't ask for what they want enough. There's this idea that if a woman's doing a good job, she will be the next one considered for a promotion or interesting assignment. It doesn't work that way though. You have to come out and ask for what you want. Men are really persistent in asking for what they want, whereas women tend to not ask, or accept it too easily if they are told 'no.'"

Women must take steps to make a good case for their request, arming themselves with as much supporting evidence, research, and information as possible. Often data and evidence can increase your bank account of negotiation bargaining chips. Negotiation always boils down to leverage, something that one of you has and the other one wants. Before any negotiation, be sure to ask yourself where and how you have leverage. Whether your leverage is your tenure, skills, education, or a combination of these factors, you need to know where your power is before walking into any negotiation.

LOOKING AHEAD: ANOTHER CASE FOR NEGOTIATION

If you are still not convinced that negotiating is a powerful and under-used tool for women's success, there is yet another case to be made for women negotiating more often. Babcock's research found that by omitting negotiation from salary discussions, a woman stands to lose more than $500,000 by age 60. This is a striking finding considering men are more than four times as likely as women to negotiate a first salary (Babcock and Laschever, 2003). A lack of negotiation does not just create negative effects in the here and now, women can also see a negative ripple effect that can hurt their financial security well into the future. Consider that your present salary effects not only your current quality of life, but also has a major impact on what wages you can ask for in subsequent jobs, and the amount both you and your employer can put into your retirement savings.

The Wage Project, Inc., a nonprofit organization dedicated to ending discrimination against women in the workplace, has done further research to quantify the amount women stand to lose by not being paid what they are worth. Compared to men they graduated with—the Wage Project found that over their lifetime—female high school graduates can lose $700,000, a female college graduate can lose $1.2 million, and a female professional school graduate can lose $2 million (www.wageproject.org). These are staggering figures, and underscore the point that it is more important than ever for women to negotiate a fair salary. Clearly where you end up has much to do with where you start out.

THE BEST PREPARATION FOR NEGOTIATING

The best way to prepare for negotiation is real-life practice. Doing so will build your confidence and give you the firsthand experience to negotiate more often, in more situations, and achieve the outcomes you set out to attain. Jeanine Becker made some excellent points about negotiating, sharing,

> I think negotiation is the most valuable training a woman can receive. I teach Negotiation at Stanford Law School and significant research shows that women do not negotiate as often as men, and when they do negotiate they often set lower targets. But the research also indicates a few critical keys to success. In research on salary

negotiations, when the women had the same information as men about market standards for a particular position, women do just as well in their negotiations. . . . The wonderful thing about this research is that it gives us insight into the solutions—if women spend the time understanding the norms and market standards, we do well. So do your research!

While practice is the best way to improve negotiation skills, training can also be helpful in this area. Law schools and business schools tend to provide some helpful instruction in negotiation, above and beyond other forms of graduate education. There are also numerous training providers in negotiation and conflict management, housed in universities and independent training companies. These can be continuing education courses or classes geared toward personal or professional enrichment. Most courses in negotiation require a component of role-playing and experiential learning. Formal training can help a woman to communicate more persuasively, to be more effective at solving problems and negotiating through conflicts, and to be a better advocate for herself when it comes to professional development, salary, and career advancement. Most important, negotiation training can help lessen anxiety around negotiating, which can be insidious if you do not take proactive steps to lessen it.

NEGOTIATING HOW-TO

Prepare

The first step in a negotiation is to prepare. I urge you to take the time before a negotiation to organize yourself from an informational standpoint, as well as to prepare emotionally. It is worth noting that walking into a negotiation without having done preparation or review of the issue at hand can be disastrous, as can spontaneous or emotion-driven negotiations. The better prepared you are in terms of the facts and your demeanor, the more successful you are likely to be.

One strategy for keeping your emotions in check is to be prepared, perhaps even over prepared, for a negotiation from an informational standpoint. Write out why you are negotiating for whatever it is, and the reasons for it. Then begin to assemble any supporting research. The more relevant research you have, the better you will feel about your argument and the more compelling your case will be. So, if you were going to ask for an assistant, for example, you might do research within your company to see what the standard criteria is for hiring an assistant. How many people does an assistant typically support? How senior does one have to be to have an assistant? What kind of revenue does a department have to produce in order to justify having an assistant?

You can also do benchmarking outside of your company to see how your competitors configure their work units and the employment of assistants. Outside of supporting research, you could also begin to think about how an assistant could help your team add or create new value for your organization. Many employers think of value in terms of numbers, so is there a way for you to quantify the value and contributions of what you are negotiating for? Get familiar and well acquainted with this research, as mastering your data will help you be more creative and improvisational on the spot. Dominique Schurman, Chief Executive Officer of Papyrus, spoke to me about preparation, noting, "The better you know your material, the easier it is to flex to the audience at hand."

KEEP YOUR COOL

Preparing emotionally for a negotiation can help you better regulate your emotions during the actual discussion. I recommend striving for a composed balance between energized and relaxed. Negotiations can feel confrontational to many women, so filling yourself with positive, empowering messages in advance of the negotiation can do you a major service. Above all else, decide that you have a place at the negotiation table and a right to ask for what you want. If you become fearful, remind yourself of what prompted you to ask for the negotiation in the first place. Separate for yourself the person you will be speaking with and the problem you are trying to solve—they are not the same. Boost yourself up emotionally by dwelling on your strengths and abilities; concentrate on several of your past successes to increase your confidence and optimism. If you exude a positive and approachable attitude going into a negotiation, you are more likely to act confidently and send the message that you are interested in both parties gaining from the discussion. This will help to put the person you are negotiating with at ease from the beginning.

I also encourage you to invite a trusted friend, partner, classmate, mentor, or colleague to role-play the negotiation with you in advance. Explain what you are planning to negotiate for and ask your associate to play the part of your negotiation counterpart. You may want to ask the role-player to be fair and balanced the first time, and to be harder to negotiate with— perhaps more critical of the request or providing more pushback—a second time and even a third time. Having someone poke holes in your argument while defending your stance will help you feel more self-assured and better equipped when it is actually time to sit down and bargain.

Another helpful strategy as you prepare to negotiate is to take the time to visualize the actual negotiation in your mind. I have used this strategy countless times for anxiety-producing events, and it has helped me every time I have used it—without fail. Instead of letting my mind go wherever it wants to before an important event, such as a negotiation, conference presentation, or sales pitch, I purposefully move myself to a quiet place where I can concentrate uninterrupted. I slowly and purposefully picture myself presenting or negotiating with ease, speaking comfortably and confidently. I build on the image, picturing the person I am negotiating with seeing my point of view and respecting me for speaking up. I picture the outcome as I would like to see it, and I see myself after the negotiation feeling pride in myself for holding my ground. The newness of a negotiation situation can add to a woman's anxiety. By taking the newness out of the situation through role-play and visualization, you will clear your mind of fear and be better able to access your best ideas during the actual negotiation. Furthermore, visualization is a technique long used by Olympic athletes for maximum performance!

One other critical area to consider is the least amount you will accept in a negotiation, and the best-case scenario for which you are striving. You will also need to decide what you will do if you get less cooperation than you had bargained for—or none at all. Are you willing to walk away if you do not get your least desired outcome? Years ago, I made the mistake of not deciding when I would walk away before a salary negotiation and subsequently accepted an offer that was below my personal preference. Because I had not established firmly in my mind when I would walk away (my drop-dead point), I did not act with the confidence or negotiation skills I could have. I was able to negotiate my salary later in my tenure at that job, but I learned the hard way that I should have negotiated a higher wage upfront and held my ground. Decide ahead of time when you will walk away or if you are even willing to. Again, the more leverage you have, the easier it will be to ask for what you want. What do you have that the counterpart you are negotiating with needs?

Negotiation Checklist

- Identify what your leverage is in the negotiation
- Role-play the negotiation at least once
- Visualize successful outcomes
- Regulate emotions
- Study research that supports your case
- Note the least you are willing to accept (worst case)
- Note the ideal state you are striving for (best case)
- Take a win-win approach: How can we both stand to gain?

Negotiate with confidence

It is critical to approach the actual negotiation with a composed, positive attitude. Again, do whatever is required to reduce your anxiety—replay your past successes in your head, think about the strength of your argument or research, and visualize the negotiation going successfully. You can begin by thanking the person for meeting with you, and even stating your confidence in the fact that you will have a fruitful discussion and arrive at a mutually beneficial solution.

While you are negotiating, use the technique of asking open-ended questions, which can be very powerful. These questions open up dialogue and can even buy you more time if you need to gather your thoughts. These questions, some examples of which are shown below, help guide and move the conversation along.

- Can you explain how you arrived at that solution?
- How are decisions like these determined?
- Are you willing to negotiate that point?
- What is keeping us from coming to an agreement?
- How could I help you feel more comfortable with this request?
- What is most important to you? Can you explain why?
- How can we move forward?
- How can we best . . . ?
- How can we make this work for both of us?
- Is that the best you can do?
- What is the cost of us not coming to an agreement?

SILENCE IS YOUR FRIEND

Silence, though not something we are well accustomed to in American culture, can be one of the greatest negotiation strategies at your disposal. When we are silent, we are not over-promising or under-selling in ways we will later regret, instead we are giving ourselves the precious gift of time and space. Silence affords us the luxury to contemplate our next move during a tricky or emotionally draining negotiation. While it can be tempting to fill in gaps in conversation, it is important to find ways to practice and get comfortable using silence.

Silence can have an effect on others as well; for one, it tends to make people uncomfortable. It can make your counterpart share information, restate their position, or try to guess what your position is. Each of these attempts to break the silence put you in a more favorable position. The strategy of silence is especially important for women to use since they may be tempted to accommodate their counterpart, fill a conversation void, or not want to seem "difficult" or withholding.

In the case of Mia, a senior manager with an international medical device company, the use of silence has worked for her with wonderful results. Since Mia's job performance is based on a Management by Objectives (MBO) approach, during her performance review she is expected to share on a 100-point scale how well she met the targets set for her a year before. In one such review, Mia explained to her boss that she thought she met her objectives at a rate of 105 percent. She had overheard her male counterparts sharing that they would request even higher rates from their bosses, so she felt her estimate was ambitious, and yet fair. Mia's boss countered her rate, challenging that he thought she met only 95 percent of her targets. Mia sat strategically silent as her boss explained himself, and as she remained silent, an interesting thing happened. Her boss seemed to become uncomfortable. He stammered and started talking himself out of his original rate of 95 percent, eventually offered her exactly what she asked for originally—105 percent.

Mia used silence in yet another powerful negotiation. After being approached by a headhunter who wanted to discuss an open position with her, Mia explained that she wanted a job in sales management, not international management as the headhunter had offered. He started to explain the benefits of taking an international assignment, however, as Mia sat silently, he began to shift his argument to better meet her needs. He ultimately suggested that a "hybrid opportunity" could be arranged that would include her preference of sales management and his preference of international work.

The next time you are in a negotiation situation, experiment with being quiet rather than speaking up right away or thanking your counterpart. Silence can give you power, as well as valuable time to process the bargaining conversation. Using silence can feel awkward at first, so I urge you to practice this technique before a negotiation.

A WIN-WIN ORIENTATION

Outside of asking powerful questions and using silence well, I recommend that you look for a way for both parties to win. Roxanne Spillett, President and Chief Executive Officer of Boys and Girls Clubs of America, shared, "One important piece of advice is to look for a 'win-win' in relationships and negotiations. Every time you think there's a 'win-loss' situation, look for ways to make it mutually beneficial. It is always better to leave something on the table in a negotiation than to walk away with everything. This is a pretty important practice as a leader." Coming up with creative solutions and concessions can certainly show your willingness to get to common ground in a negotiation. Use questions to understand your counterpart's needs, and then reiterate those needs and look for a way they can be met, preferably without your conceding something. If you must concede something, negotiate to get something else back. Since women are adept at reading body language and nonverbal communication, I recommend leveraging that skill to interpret cues such as discomfort or concern.

I also suggest you clarify the positions once they have been finalized by mirroring back what you heard. Even if you need to have another conversation or get information from a third party, I still advise that you sum up what was discussed. For example, "So to summarize, you are comfortable with me reducing my hours to 20 hours per week and moving to an hourly rate of my current salary. However, you need to double-check with human resources on whether or not my 401K will be affected and then you'll get back to me." This will give both of you a chance to focus your thinking, minimize misunderstandings, and make any clarifications if something was misunderstood. I also suggest that you put it in writing, such as in a follow-up e-mail. That way, if your counterpart denies the terms of the negotiation (or altogether leaves the company), you have some form of proof of your discussion. Finally, thank your counterpart for his or her efforts to find common ground and for his or her willingness to discuss the matter with you.

Following are several common workplace situations where women are in a position to negotiate more often. With each of these situations, I have included specific advice to help you navigate similar situations in your own job.

NEGOTIATING SALARY WHEN YOU GET A JOB OFFER

As we have already discovered, the implications of negotiating, or not negotiating, your salary can be great. Avoiding salary negotiation can have a negative domino effect on your current and future earning potential. The Institute for Women's Policy Research (IWPR) found the ratio of women's to men's median weekly earnings for full-time workers was 79.9 percent in 2008, the third consecutive decline since the historical high of 81.0 percent in 2005 (2009). If this makes you as frustrated as it makes me, I urge you to ask for what you deserve, and disagree with your boss or human resources contact if you do not receive it.

First, I would suggest that you avoid bringing up money until the company really wants to hire you. You have far more leverage in a salary negotiation when a company's hiring team is enthusiastic about you and feels you are "it." When it is time to talk money, I would advise you to evade the question, "What you are currently making?" As the employer, the onus is on them to provide you with a salary range, not the other way around. Furthermore, by answering the question about your current salary, you can lose a major salary bargaining chip. You might instead want to say that money is not your first priority, that what matters more is the company, its values, and the job itself. Of course, avoiding answering the salary question can be awkward at times since you can feel you are dodging a question, but that is exactly the point. If you must give a number, I suggest either giving a broad range or giving a figure that encompasses your entire compensation package, inclusive of your bonus and benefits.

I would also be sure to do some solid research before engaging in salary talks. Why? Babcock's research has found that women often undervalue their contributions and work. Her research showed that women's salary expectations are 3 to 32 percent lower than those of men with the same jobs. As such, do your research; there are many places you can find salary information. Some general information can be obtained from salary Web sites, while other sources can include data you find from industry associations or schools you have attended. For example, a salary survey was conducted during the first year of the MBA program I attended, and I used the results as one more data point to justify my pay increase. You can also bring in figures you have been quoted from headhunters or other hiring professionals. Networking contacts can also give you ballpark salary figures, and some may even tell you what their salary history has looked like.

If for some reason you cannot negotiate the salary you want, do not be shy about asking for other concessions. You might ask if you can have a better title, and be prepared with examples you like. Consider asking for an additional week of vacation time or other benefits, such as help with relocation costs or funds for professional development, training, or tuition.

ANNUAL PERFORMANCE REVIEWS

Annual performance reviews are such an important event for women that I would put this section in flashing lights if I could! Many individuals, men and women alike, dread these annual or bi-annual meetings with their bosses. Numerous clients I have worked with tell me that they walk into their annual review meeting feeling apprehensive, without doing a single thing to prepare, and allow their bosses to simply lead the conversations to their final destination.

I recommend taking a very different approach . . . The very first thing I suggest doing is to be an active participant in your performance review.

Come prepared with your own agenda of topics you would like to cover and any supporting documents you would like to share with your boss. In addition, I suggest you keep a list of professional successes, projects you have spearheaded, and improvements you have made throughout the year. It is rare that a person can remember all of her achievements after a busy year, so rather than handicapping yourself by forgetting accomplishments, keep an ongoing log. Be creative in what you jot down, and remember to include projects you have personally spearheaded and concrete tasks you have completed, in addition to any other supporting evidence that could help you to get a favorable review, a promotion, or an increase in your salary. If you can quantify your accomplishments, all the better; metrics are the common language of business. Barbara A. F. Greene, Chief Executive Officer of Greene and Associates, Inc., supports this idea, recommending "[P]romote yourself more. We think people will recognize our hard work, but you have to be visible and advocate for what you need."

One of the most effective strategies I have used in my own career is to keep track of the accolades and praise that I receive. After the conclusion of a project, if I receive an e-mail from an executive saying that I was instrumental in the project's success, I file it in an area where I can quickly grab it later. I do the same with verbal praise I might receive, noting whom it was from and what exactly was shared. Remember, bosses have short memories! It is your job, therefore, to surface all of your accomplishments and remind your boss about your value. Jamie McCourt confirmed this need to share our achievements when she noted, "Women need to be more outspoken about their accomplishments." Show your boss that you know what kind of value you are creating for the organization.

NEGOTIATING FOR ADVANCEMENT

Performance reviews represent a perfect, structured time to bring up career growth. These meetings are a great time to ask for advancement opportunities, such as managing a high-visibility project, assuming a "stretch" task that pushes you out of your daily routine, or taking a challenging rotational assignment. It is crucial for women to make it known if they want to advance. Illustrating this point was Naomi C. Earp when I asked her what strategy for advancing a career goes overlooked most. She simply noted, "Asking for what we want." You can succeed on the job in many different ways, but you have to get comfortable making requests of other people, particularly your boss.

Whether you are seeking a special assignment, a formal promotion, a new title, or a raise—ask for it! Denise Incandela, President of Saks Direct at Saks Fifth Avenue, encouraged, "Don't be afraid to approach your boss and tell him or her that you're ready for more responsibility. Clearly communicate your career aspirations and then work with your boss to develop an action plan that will build your experience and skill set so that you can be ready for your next role." By discussing your advancement and development, you are conveying to your boss that you are hungry, ambitious, and not satisfied with the status quo. After stating your career goals, I recommend asking for an action plan or other pointed advice as to how you can actually attain your goal. Your boss can help you craft explicit steps to reaching your goals, and can also serve as a culture guide who can help you understand the more nuanced, and often hidden rules of advancing.

NEGOTIATING FOR A RAISE

In one particularly revealing study performed by Babcock and her team, Babcock convened 74 student volunteers to play the word game Boggle. Before engaging in the game, the volunteers were told they would be paid between $3 and $10 for their participation. The participants played the game, after which Babcock and her team gave each participant $3. Participants were asked if the $3 was acceptable. Male students were eight times more likely than female students to ask for more money. Even when Babcock tried the experiment in a different way, in which she stipulated that the sum of $3 to $10 was negotiable, the difference between male students and female students was striking: 83 percent of the male students asked for more money while only 58 percent of the female students did. When the female students were told that negotiation was acceptable, more of them actually bargained for a higher sum (Small, Gelfand, Babcock, & Gettman, 2005). However, the practice of asking for what we want is still alien to many women. Undeniably, this is a factor that we must move beyond if we want to be fully represented at the top of organizations.

I recommend negotiating squarely with your boss for increased pay if you believe you are undervalued or under-compensated. Your belief, of course, should be supported by data and evidence. If, for example, you were going to ask for a raise at your present company, you might research salary Web sites, the U.S. Department of Labor's statistics, salary data from industry associations you belong to, salary statistics from schools or universities, and anecdotal salary information you have heard from others. If headhunters call you about job opportunities, you should also include those figures if they support your case.

Outside of supporting research, you could also begin to think about how you add or create value for your organization. Remember that the more irreplaceable you are and the more unique and needed your skill set, the more value you represent for your company. Since many employers think of value in terms of numbers, how can you quantify your value and contributions? Get well acquainted with your research, as mastering your data will help you be more creative and articulate on the spot. Also, conduct a comparison of your job description compared to your actual duties. If you are going to succeed in a negotiation, you have to believe you are worth the extra investment. As you would in any negotiation, approach the situation in a positive way, confident that an agreement can be reached.

I advise tackling the situation with an approach of being solution-focused, not complaining or negative. For example, you can project the tone of, "I love my job and feel well matched to my department and the company, but . . ." I would also do your homework specific to your company in advance of any meetings so that you are well equipped. Research the standard pay practices of your company, including human resource policies, so that you know the company protocol on such matters. If you do this, often times you will be more knowledgeable about your company's position on raises than your boss is! Educate yourself on whether or not employees get increases once a year or if they are eligible for adjustments more often. Going through this exercise will help you know if what you are asking for is an exception or a rule and you can present it accordingly. This information in combination with your market research will be invaluable in your bargaining conversation.

In the event your negotiation does not go as you would like, I do not recommend leveling an ultimatum at your boss or threatening to quit. Instead, express your honest disappointment and keep the remainder of the conversation solution-focused. Ask when the soonest is that you can become eligible for a raise. If you continue to believe you are undervalued or undercompensated, consider looking for a job elsewhere.

A summary of salary negotiation steps is noted below:

1. Set the context: "I'd like to discuss my future with you."
2. Lay the foundation: "This is how I see my work currently."
3. Differentiate yourself: "This is how I am unique and indispensable."
4. Supplement with research: "Here is some supporting research regarding salaries in my field."
5. Make the request: "Considering what I've laid out for you, I am requesting . . ."
6. Thank you: "I appreciate your time and consideration."

NEGOTIATING WHEN YOU EXPERIENCE "JOB CREEP"

You should also consider using the art of negotiation if you experience "job creep." Job creep occurs when your daily work duties spread significantly outside of the bounds of your job description. Job creep can also occur when you are dispatched by phone, e-mail, or other connections typically during off-work hours. If you are uncomfortable with the direction your job is taking, either because of the time commitment or a mounting workload, it is up to you to constructively explain the situation to your boss and negotiate for a different arrangement.

Before taking any action, however, consider why you are experiencing job creep. Is it because your job duties have doubled in number? Is it because you have three new team members that require constant mentoring? It is especially important to discern if the job creep you are experiencing is because of work assignments being given to you, or if you have a personal responsibility in the job creep. For some people, their procrastination or inefficient use of work time can create job creep. Take the time to tease apart what aspects of your job creep are in your control versus your boss's. Also, if you have the authority, try delegating some of your work before approaching your boss. Delegation shows that you are a trusting manager, and that you know what duties are essential to complete but not necessarily by you.

If you do sit down to discuss your workload with your boss, keep the conversation positive and focused on your intention to deliver top-notch work. Lora J. Villarreal, Ph.D., Executive Vice President and Chief People Officer at Affiliated Computer Services, Inc. (ACS), suggests, "If you're over your limit, talk to your boss, tell them what you're working on since they may have forgotten, and tell them you're afraid to sacrifice the quality of your work. You can say, 'I can handle this—but it won't be an "A" day from me.' Then let them decide what to do." By positioning your workload matter as a potential threat to quality work, it shows your boss that you take pride and ownership in the level of work you do. You might also try a line such as, "I know how important the X account is, and I want to make sure that what we deliver is top-notch. Right now, I am concerned that will not happen given the workload I'm carrying. Together, can we find a creative way to manage this?" If your boss decides he or she does not want anything taken off your plate, ask if there is any work that could be shared, or if you can get the assistance of a temp or support staff.

NEGOTIATING FOR PROFESSIONAL DEVELOPMENT OR JOB RESOURCES

We will not always have the exact elements in a job that we want. However, that does not mean we cannot ask for all the things we want. Whether you want to go to a training or a conference or get a degree, there are many resources that you can negotiate for your employer to support or subsidize. Just as I have already covered throughout this chapter, you will need to assemble a case for your negotiation request with pertinent facts and evidence. If there is training you would like to attend, for example, find out how much the training will cost and what the benefits of attending are. Then take these generalized benefits and figure out what company- or department-specific benefits your employer will see from your attending. Share the relevance of your training with your manager. Use the angle of staying current in your field and keeping abreast of competitors' activity as supplemental reasons to go.

DeeDee Wilson, Chief Financial Officer at Aritzia, shared a valuable story on this very topic. She recalled, "About ten years ago, I saw an opportunity to take a leadership course but the cost was $2,500. I hesitated to ask my boss if I could go, and when I finally did, he said 'yes.' Years after attending this training, I still find myself using the principles I learned repeatedly." You are worth your company's investment of time, money, and support. Find the courage to ask for the growth opportunities you want and, like all negotiations, fortify your appeal with facts.

NEGOTIATING WHEN YOU DISAGREE

You may use negotiation to bargain, make a case, or ask for what you want. You may also negotiate as a means to articulate the merit of your ideas, or to argue against taking a direction you think is wrong. Catherine J. Mathis, Senior Vice President of Corporate Communications at The New York Times Company, noted, "If you don't say no, you won't move up. When you have to go against the current, you will need courage and conviction. You have to stay true to who you are and speak your mind; otherwise, you won't succeed." Using negotiation when you do not agree with something is critical, as you will need to trust your deepest held ethics and values, knowledge, and skills. You will also need to listen to your gut instinct. Courteney Monroe commented on listening to her instincts and shared, "I always listen to them and when I don't, I regret it. My gut has served me so well that the one percent of the time I don't listen to it, I wish I had."

What if you advocate for something and do not get what you want? Melissa M. Monk, Chief Infrastructure Officer at Capital One remembered, "There are explicit events, like when I didn't get a promotion or job I thought I deserved. Those have been real inflection points for me. There have also been times when my ideas were not accepted. If I really believe in an idea, I try to figure out a way to recommunicate the message so that its value comes through. Failure is part of progress toward success; no one consistently gets it right the first time." Melissa's comment about repackaging a point to appeal to people differently is an excellent one. Perhaps your message just needs fine-tuning, positioning, or more data to back it up. If your negotiation skills or the larger environment you are working in cannot get you where you want to be, there may be times when you will have to let the issue die altogether.

GO FOR IT!

Negotiating, or asking for what you want, seems simple to do, but it is harder than it sounds for many women. The reality, however, is that women already negotiate every day—whether it is working out decisions with bosses, deciding on the division of labor at home with a partner, or assigning duties to get a project completed with peers. The most important message here is that we need to build a bridge from the everyday negotiations we already engage in to those in the workplace.

The women I interviewed had a comfort and ease when it came to asking for what they want, pointing to the fact that being a leader requires asking for tangible resources, more funds in the budget, another staff member, or advocating for an alternate direction for the organization. DeeDee Wilson remembered, "I've never been afraid to say, 'This is what I want and why, and this is how I plan to deliver on it.' If I was told 'no' the first time, I would go back and ask several more times. You need to take what you want!" Negotiation will almost never hurt you, rather almost always help. You do not need to love negotiating, but you must understand how the rules of negotiation work in order to play the game effectively. See negotiating as a collaboration or forum, not a winner-loser type competition. And remember, if you negotiate, you are more likely to get what you ask for!

Maneuvering Through
Office Politics

POLITICS AT WORK

What are office politics and why do they have any bearing on one's leadership abilities? Politics are the often unspoken, unshared rules of how things get done in an organization. While the term "office politics" has a negative connotation and can be associated with terms such as "opportunistic," "crafty," or "manipulative," politics are not necessarily toxic or bad. Politics are merely the dynamics formed by leadership and the workforce that are unique to a given company. Since politics control a large amount of decision making, it is important to understand how to identify significant political players, how to tailor your communication style to your organization's culture, and how to mobilize a group to effect change. Just as important is learning strategies for fostering meritocracy and identifying when politics cross over to ethical breaches.

Samuel B. Bacharach, Director of Cornell University's Institute for Workplace Studies, defined political competence aptly in his book *Get Them on Your Side* as the "ability to understand what you can and cannot control, when to take action, who is going to resist your agenda, and whom you need on your side. It's about knowing how to map the political terrain and get others on your side, as well as lead coalitions" (Bacharach, 2005). Bacharach's explanation of political competence encompasses perceptiveness as well as relationship and change management.

Just as any group has distinct dynamics based on the makeup of its members, so too do complex systems and organizations. These dynamics are not necessarily formed knowingly, however. Politics are shaped by people's intended or unintended behaviors and actions, and are one component of the larger, pervading corporate culture. In my personal view, politics are neither positive nor negative; they just "are." Leaders are affected by politics because their success can depend in part on how well they work within their organizational framework, with different personalities, and within the cultural rules of their company.

Political tactics are not an area that we typically learn about in school, college, or graduate programs. And yet based on the interviews I conducted, those women that get ahead have the perceptiveness to see how politics work at their organization. They accept that politics exist in every entity and spend the time to acquaint themselves with the particular dynamics of each company where they work. The women I met with recognize who holds power and influence in their organization and how people prefer to get information delivered. They are also savvy about when and how to challenge authority.

BACKGROUND ON CULTURE

In looking at office politics, it is important to consider culture and how politics fit into the larger, political framework. Edgar Schein, a pioneer in organizational development, described the culture of a group as:

> A pattern of shared basic assumptions that the group learned as it solved its problems of external adaptation and internal integration, that has worked well enough to be considered valid, and, therefore, to be taught to new members as the correct way to perceive, think, and feel in relation to these problems.

Schein elucidates that culture is comprised of three primary levels: Artifacts, Espoused Values, and Basic Underlying Assumptions. Politics can permeate from each of these levels, particularly within Espoused Values and Basic Underlying Assumptions (2004). Artifacts represent the tangible symbols and processes which people can see, feel, or hear. Employees use such symbols to understand what to subscribe to, from corporate logos and products to terminology and dress code. The second level of culture, Espoused Values, represents the stated philosophies, goals and strategies that an organization projects. These expressions can take the form of mission statements, mottos, and value statements, an area that becomes problematic if there is a difference between stated and lived values. The third level is an organization's Basic Underlying Assumptions. This level is formed by the actual behaviors that people consistently demonstrate and is often invisible to those within a system. This level can be a major indicator of culture and politics as it reflects the subtle demonstration of the dominant styles, preferences, and learned beliefs of an organization.

Politics and culture are certainly interrelated and can be equally challenging for organizations to change. Ingrained habits and behaviors can be part of the cultural and political functioning in nuanced, hard to notice ways. The key as an individual is to be open and perceptive to learning how your workplace operates, from what is espoused to what values are actually lived. Donna Callejon, Chief Operating Officer of GlobalGiving, suggests looking at culture sooner rather than later, "Try to get a good read early in a job on the organizational culture. . . . Younger men and women are used to their ideas being welcomed, or even actively sought-out by their parents and others, but this isn't necessarily the case in a top-down organization." Donna's point reinforces that culture can be important in knowing when, how, and to whom your message should be delivered.

LEARNING YOUR ORGANIZATION'S POLITICS

Many people overlook politics and their importance in getting work done. This is a deadly career mistake; doing so can make you more vulnerable to surprises, attacks, or missed career opportunities. Even if you are highly intelligent and have numerous contributions to bring to your organization, your efforts could be futile if you do not know *how* your entity functions. Familiarizing yourself with the cultural underpinnings of your organization's politics is not possible to do in your first week, however; learning how your organization operates takes time. Erin McGinnis, National Committee Chair of the Society of Women Engineers, recommends, "I think it can take 6–9 months just to learn the culture of a company and . . . what is seen as important and what isn't." The amount of time it takes you to learn about your organization will vary, but if you are conscious about learning and open to what you find, you will get faster and more perceptive over time at mastering office politics. Consider the questions below as you orient yourself to your political environment and assess how things work:

- What symbols does the company use to convey their values? Are the symbols and values actually lived?
- How is power dispersed? Is the environment top-down and hierarchical, or is power more diffused?
- Who are the people of greatest influence?
- Does the company's public brand match the internal brand?
- In what style do people speak? Formally or casually? Is there technical or industry jargon that people use?

- How openly do people speak? How relaxed or conservative is the environment?
- How do people stay informed about company news? What is the standard protocol for getting and giving information?
- Can people ask questions freely? Can people disagree publicly with a decision or direction?
- What nonverbal cues do people use to convey information?
- How do people dress? How else do people present themselves?
- How is your boss seen by the company? What is your boss's reputation within the company?
- How is your department seen? Is it well established or new? What is your department's reputation within the company?

Since many companies espouse one thing in writing but actually live another set of values, it is important to look at facts as well as less tangible data as you make your assessment. Asking and answering the questions above will give you a clear professional advantage over those who take a passive approach to learning about their organization. The process of discovery in answering these questions will help you be more astute about the culture and politics of the workplace, which will help you to be more productive sooner in your tenure. Taking a proactive, open approach to organizational learning helps you to be perceptive early on, allowing you to do your work in line with the company style and practice, and giving you the ability to produce more work at a faster rate from the time you start.

By engaging in the critical process of culture orientation, I do not want to suggest that you should learn about your company culture merely to mimic it and conform to the culture. Rather I think it is vital to be *aware* and *perceptive* of the politics. Blindly mirroring your company's politics is not an approach that will move you or your company forward. I encourage you to find a balance with office culture and politics where you can speak the language of your organization, influence change, engage stakeholders, and bring new perspectives and insights to light.

The political learning curve you will need to embark upon within each new job requires you to hone multiple skills. Naomi C. Earp, Chair of the U.S. Equal Employment Opportunity Commission (EEOC), articulated this political learning curve, saying, "Listening and looking for the silent, nonverbal cues [has served me particularly well when navigating organizational politics]. A lot of a company's culture is not spoken—how people dress, how meetings are conducted, who has power—there are always unwritten rules. After you listen, you need to ask questions." As perceptive as you are to implicit and explicit messages at your company, you will also need input from people on how the organization functions. I encourage you to seek different people out to create a patchwork of learning, rather than listening narrowly to only one specific group or person.

AN INCLUSIVE APPROACH

Supporting the need to get a well informed "culture orientation," Jeanine Becker, Senior Counsel at Motorola, Inc., notes, "When I just join an organization, I value taking the time to understand the politics and spend that initial time just getting familiar with how things work. I also seek input from many sources and get different perspectives on the politics before jumping in." Jeanine makes an extremely useful point: taking an inclusive approach to learning about people and culture will serve you better than relying on a single stream of information. Inclusivity is also an approach to work that recognizes the importance of others' contributions whether they are from other cultures or genders or other departments or business units. Alexandra Miller, Chief Executive Officer of Mercedes Medical, Inc., explained to me, "As I get older, I challenge the conclusions that have failed me in the past. Your instincts, especially in business, are not always right. One has to be inclusive on business decisions these days in order to make the right decision."

You can maximize your learning by seeking out and speaking with many sources at your company. Doing this will also help you in other ways: you will make more friends, build more alliances, and develop a rapport with those you may work with in the future. Do not make the mistake of aligning yourself with one person or faction at your company. Doing so can prematurely brand you in a way that does not help you. Remember, high performance people and teams benefit from diversity of thought.

INTERNAL CUSTOMER SERVICE

As mentioned in Chapter 3, taking an internal customer service approach is one of the best ways to build your personal brand and to fortify yourself to better handle politics in the future. Ultimately, internal customer service means serving those in your organization just as well as you would your best customer. I recommend that you actually view your coworkers' requests as you would customers', treating them accordingly, rather than as a drain on your time or a nuisance. Furthermore, I suggest you do this without regard to title, rank, or hierarchy. If you gain a reputation for delivering strong results with a great attitude, it will be hard for people *not* to get word of it. So few people treat their coworkers as VIPs, that those who do stand out immeasurably.

Taking an internal customer service approach is also one of the most overlooked ways to gain friends and allies at work. Doing so will leave a positive legacy and imprint of you at the company, even after you have left. Denise Incandela, President of Saks Direct at Saks Fifth Avenue, said, "Getting people vested in my success has helped me navigate politics. It has allowed me to build my network from a broad spectrum within my organization. I try to treat colleagues like they are customers. If you do that, your coworkers should become advocates of yours." Denise's point emphasizes another important angle. Many of those whom you serve internally will have more power or influence than you do. By showing them that you are smart, considerate, and approachable, you will make them want to advocate for your success in the future. Giving your teammates VIP treatment can yield you promotions and choice assignments, as news of your excellent internal customer service skills will travel around the organization. Model your interactions with colleagues with the attitude that you are happy to serve them, and your positive reputation will grow!

POSITIVE, SOLUTION-ORIENTED PEOPLE GO FURTHER

Along with an internal customer service approach, you can also build political capital by taking a cooperative, solution-focused approach to work. Said Denise Incandela, "I recommend that you work to over-deliver on your projects, be positive and solution-oriented, and that you get as many people vested in your career advancement as soon as possible." Why does being positive and solution-focused matter? For one thing, people want to be around those who are positive and lift them up. Positive people have a magnetizing effect and their approach tends to dissipate conflict and emotional charge. Positive people also focus more often on what can be, rather than what is. Since problem-solvers are needed in every single industry, a can-do attitude goes a long way. Supporting this point, Alexandra Miller recommends, "Stay positive—this is not a platitude—you will have to learn this skill. People are drawn to and want to be around positive people. That translates to business success."

As you consider what kind of approach you take at work, carefully evaluate what kind of footprint you would like to leave on the organization. Positive people will almost always leave a better legacy than pessimists who are a drain on morale and productivity. As Rosslyn Kleeman, Chair of the Coalition for Effective Change, rightly noted, "Be sure to be positive. There is nothing worse at work than sour people. Don't be a downer!"

An optimistic attitude can also help you more quickly rebound from project failures or mistakes. Rather than getting mired in the failure itself, optimistic people are better able to quickly pick themselves up and learn an important lesson for next time. Daniel Goleman, Ph.D., the esteemed psychologist, lecturer, author, and consultant on emotional intelligence, noted, "People who are optimistic see a failure as due to something that can be changed so that they can succeed next time around, while pessimists take the blame for the failure, ascribing it to some characteristic they are helpless to change" (1998). So much of staying flexible reduces to seeing obstacles as inevitable, and yet surmountable.

EMOTIONAL INTELLIGENCE LEADS TO BETTER UNDERSTANDING THE ORGANIZATION

Outside of being vigilant and perceptive in your environment, you can also use your own self-knowledge to improve your standing at work. This includes leveraging your emotional intelligence, a useful skill when it comes to office politics. So what is emotional intelligence? The work of Daniel Goleman points to the fact that technical intelligence does not indicate success at work as much as we once thought. Rather, emotional intelligence—the process of recognizing our own feelings and those of others, motivating ourselves, and managing our emotions—accounts for a far larger piece of what is required for leadership.

In his book *Working with Emotional Intelligence,* Goleman found some differences in emotional intelligence between men and women highlighting, "Women, on average, tend to be more aware of their emotions, show more empathy, and are more adept interpersonally" (1998). Many interviewees echoed a similarly positive sentiment about women, explaining that women are naturals at reading people and situations. I recommend that you maximize any skills you may have in emotional intelligence as a means to understand and maneuver through office politics. Shannon S. S. Herzfeld, Vice President of Government Relations at Archer Daniels Midland Company, shares, "Politics are easier to manage when you have a good sense of people and are a good listener. You have to go beyond words to key into how people are feeling. Interestingly, the same qualities that have made me a good mother have made me a good executive."

According to those I interviewed, there is a clear connection between emotional intelligence and maneuvering successfully through office politics. Autumn Bayles, Senior Vice President of Strategic Operations at Tasty Baking Company, noted, "It's a real art. The more emotional intelligence you have, the better you will be at navigating politics. You need to use your influence to sell your ideas, and I think many women are naturally good at this." While men have certain areas of emotional intelligence in which they are especially strong, such as self-confidence, optimism, and adaptability (Goleman, 1998), women should use any dominant skills to their full advantage. If you are good at reading a room, for example, including body language and other silent cues, use those skills to your benefit next time you are in a contentious meeting or negotiation.

Highlighting yet another angle of emotional intelligence, Maya Rockeymoore, Ph.D., President and Founder of Global Policy Solutions, recommends, "Learn about yourself, be a student of yourself. Understand your organization's context and people and figure out when it is or isn't about you. Understand what drives action. Figure out what you need to get out of a job and remember that water cooler relationships can be more important than you think." If you are open and honest with yourself about your own contributions and strengths, you will be more effective at leveraging those same strengths intrapersonally and for the benefit of the entire organization. Self-awareness can certainly make you more sophisticated at negotiating politics.

Dr. Rockeymoore also shares that a critical aspect of maneuvering through politics is learning to note when situations are or are not about you. There will always be undercurrents and situations that do not involve you at work. By keeping politics nonpersonal and about the larger group dynamic, you can more easily rise above it. I recommend looking at politics in a neutral, clinical way as you observe how work gets done. By reviewing and answering the questions below you can continue to assess important dynamics of your workplace.

Critical Questions

- How confident am I in the reliability of the information I receive? From whom do I get information?
- Who has power here?
- What do people with power have in common?
- What are the unspoken rules around here?
- In which areas does the company say one thing but do another? In what ways are there duplicity or contradictory messages and actions?
- How do key people like to be communicated with?
- Who has influence?
- Who has key contacts?
- How are mistakes or failures handled?
- How do people with influence get more influence "bargaining chips"?
- What do I need from this job?

GOOD AND BAD GOSSIP

As you make sense of the workplace politics around you and collect more information, you will need to distinguish when you are compiling information versus engaging in gossip. Gossip, generally speaking, is the trivial workplace talk that spreads sensational or intimate matters around the office. Denise Incandela recommended, "Don't get involved in negativity or gossip—to me that just embodies professional immaturity. Of course, a good rule of thumb is to only say things about people that you would say to their face[s]." I have heard Denise's rule of thumb framed for written communications as well: "Don't write anything in a work email that you wouldn't be comfortable with the whole office seeing." Discretion at work matters because leaders have to keep all kinds of data and information confidential throughout the course of their jobs. Even if you are tempted to gossip, I recommend against it. Whether secretaries, security guards, or vice presidents, you simply do not know where the things you say will travel. Remember there is no safe place for gossip, so avoid it!

D'Arcy Foster Rudnay, Senior Vice President for Comcast Corporation, also noted, "I never gossip. Gossip is dangerous and is the easiest way to get in trouble. It's also an easy way to lose respect from men. On the other hand, there is a certain type of gossip that is essential when it comes to keeping the channels of communications open with other staff members." D'Arcy underscores an earlier point: there is difference between gathering information and gossiping. Many executives have people in their organization that act as their eyes and ears. As an aspiring executive, you will likely seek out similar information to stay informed as you move up the ladder. For example, you might ask a trusted peer or subordinate, "What is your sense about how people are feeling given the news of the merger?" or "How do you think its going for people as they get used to the new sales software?" Expressing genuine interest is not a form of gossip, but a way to stay informed. Doing so is also reflective of an inclusive approach to the workplace where you ask multiple stakeholders about their perceptions and experiences. When you gather information for constructive, non-gossip purposes, you will find that most people will be flattered that you want their opinion.

DATING AT WORK

When I asked Kelly Pickett, a senior manager at a management consulting firm, "What strategy for advancing one's career goes overlooked most?" she noted, "Being professional. . . . Don't casual-date people at work. It doesn't take much for people to look at a woman in her twenties and say 'that girl has a lot of growing up to do.' You don't want to give them any more reasons to think this way." Can a woman date coworkers without hurting her reputation? Yes and no. I agree with Kelly that casual dating is a bad idea at work. When it comes to more serious dating, however, I do think it is acceptable to date coworkers provided you are honest with yourself about what you are getting into. It is also critical that the person you want to date is not in your immediate department or does not have a reporting relationship to you. I encourage you to approach dating at work extremely carefully and with good common sense. If a relationship does not work out, the reality of interacting with your ex every day can be messy and uncomfortable and lead to you being less productive on the job.

Another challenging aspect of dating at work is that it can give you the wrong kind of attention, as Kelly aptly pointed out. The reality is that your credibility and reputation are very important—and yet fragile—particularly if you are young and female. Credibility can translate to having more influence and say at work, allowing you to manage politics more aptly. Credibility can take a long time to build and very little time to destroy; treat your credibility as precious and delicate. Do not let something such as casual dating destroy what you have worked hard to build.

THE EVER IMPORTANT RELATIONSHIP WITH YOUR BOSS

Generally speaking, your relationship with your boss is absolutely critical to navigating politics and achieving more success. Your rapport with your boss is important because your boss can be your biggest advocate, acting as a motor that propels you or your heaviest anchor in terms of job advancement. In my opinion your boss can be one of the best "culture guides" at your organization, giving you inside knowledge into how things really operate. Cynthia Egan, President of Retirement Plan Services at T. Rowe Price, reiterated this idea: "You have to understand what the politics are at your particular company, because people just entering the workforce can be naïve about the extent that politics control decisions. Each organization has its own personality so you need to identify what that personality is, decide if you want to exist in it, and have good mentors or relationships to help you navigate through it. Being an island won't help you navigate politics." Your boss can be fundamental in helping you maneuver skillfully through a political labyrinth. Consider the questions below as you cultivate and steward the relationship with your boss, and think about how your boss can be a political mentor:

- How do you think your boss is seen in the organization?
- How does your boss believe he or she is seen?
- How does your boss like to get information?
- With whom is your boss allied?
- With whom does your boss have conflict?
- How has your boss garnered internal support to make a change happen?
- Whom does your boss see as reliable at your company? Why?

As you learn the answers to these questions, I recommend that you always approach the relationship with your boss from a professional stance. I suggest avoiding an overly casual relationship, which can make the line of professionalism difficult to locate at times. I also advise against becoming especially close to your boss, as friendship can make the supervisor-subordinate relationship messy and confusing. Keeping your relationship respectful and professional is your best relationship strategy. Carla E. Lucchino, Assistant Deputy Commandant, Installations and Logistics at the U.S. Marine Corps, recommends, "Having a strong relationship with your boss can really help you be successful. I look to my bosses to give me a lot of responsibility, to trust me, and [to] be a good advisor."

Outside of delivering outstanding work, one of the best things you can do to strengthen your professional relationship with your boss is to become needed and relied upon. You may even want to express this openly in a one-on-one meeting or annual review with your boss by saying, "I want you to feel you can rely on me, even if you are not here. What else can I be doing to help you see things that way?" The very process of expressing this to your boss will likely buy you some credibility. Another small but powerful strategy you can use is to show your boss what you have done while he or she was away. Whether they like it or not, many bosses do not see top productivity levels from their staff when they are out of the office. You can distinguish yourself and build trust with your boss by doing a little bit more than you are naturally inclined to on those days your boss is gone. Putting in extra effort while your boss is away is one more way you can support him or her and make your department look good. It is also one more way that you will stand out above others, since very few people think to do more rather than less when their boss is away.

BUILDING ALLIANCES AND FRIENDSHIPS

No matter how much focus we are taught to put on our technical competence at work, I would argue that our professional relationships matter just as much. Even if you have a strong relationship with your boss, most of us need even more allies to get our agendas met. Relationships at work can take the form of networks and mentor-mentee relationships, which I have already discussed, and it also includes friendships and alliances. While friendships at work bring you enjoyment and camaraderie, workplace alliances differ slightly. Allies are mutually beneficial relationships that help members to accomplish their goals and realize their ideas at work. While an ally may also be your friend, an ally should ultimately provide you with professional help, whether through good advice, a unique or different perspective on the company, or the technical knowledge to help you solve your problems. Just as you would with a mentor, keep your promises, act professionally, give credit where it is due, and make sure the relationship is two-way. I suggest looking for ways that you can help remove barriers for your allies.

Truly good alliances last even after one person leaves the company. This not only can help your alliance to flower and benefit from more perspectives, but it also builds your network. Allies do not need to be at your exact level in an organization for both of you to derive value from the relationship. The main requirements for successful alliances are that you trust each other, you support each other, and you both stand to benefit. Even if you have received significant support from your ally and it is not apparent how you could return the favor, always offer anyway. A genuine offer to return the favor will engender appreciation and mutual respect, and will steward the relationship for a need one of you may have in the future.

One reality of alliance-building is that it is easier to do when you are likeable. Your interpersonal skills will always have a bearing on how hard people want to work for you or how much they want to work with you. Even if extraversion is not natural to you, it helps to make people feel comfortable and at ease. Courteney Monroe, Executive Vice President of Consumer Marketing at HBO, shared, "I have the personality for navigating politics. I know how to relate to different kinds of people and make them comfortable. Generally speaking, people need to like you if you're going to move up. You need to make people feel that you understand them." Furthering this point, in Tim Sanders' book *The Likeability Factor: How to Boost Your L-Factor and Achieve Your Life's Dreams,* Sanders notes that likeable people have the best chances of being hired, promoted, and rewarded. Likeability was so important, in fact, that in Sanders' research, it ranked above traits such as drive, ambition, self-confidence, and intelligence (2006).

Adding to this idea, Cathy Fleming, Partner at Nixon Peabody LLP, made an interesting point about diffusing political charge with levity, citing, "Having a sense of humor and being able to laugh at myself and my situation has served me well. It also helps to have people skills when it comes to navigating politics." D'Arcy Foster Rudnay also emphasized the importance of humor, noting, "Be smart without being obnoxious. Having a sense of humor is important . . . especially if you want to have camaraderie with men."

BECOME A CHANGE AGENT

Change is such a big challenge in organizations that full-time staff and outside management consultants are paid millions of dollars each year to facilitate it. Change is inherently complex and nebulous organizationally, but it is possible to do. Interestingly, change on a small scale follows a similar general process as change on a grand scale. If there is an issue, a cause, or an initiative that you want to rally for at work, consider a "change management" strategy as you implement your cause. Patricia Deyton, Director of the Center for Gender in Organizations at Simmons School of Management, recommended, "First understand the politics, including who has power, connections, and influence. Engage in these politics in a positive way. Create a coalition to make change happen with like-minded people and always be transparent about your motivations." Using your influence to harness positive change is one of the best things you can do to leave a favorable legacy at your company.

Consider the change steps below, which can serve you in a repeatable way across many change initiatives:

1. **Define the Baseline:** Demonstrate how the current state of the situation you want to change is affecting the company, the staff, the customers, or any other stakeholders.
2. **Solicit Input:** Begin to stimulate people's thinking by involving them in round-table discussions, townhall-style meetings, or even focus groups. Involving others in coming up with solutions to problems is a great way to foster buy-in.
3. **Generate Excitement:** Build momentum and enthusiasm toward change by communicating progress with people and reinvolving them when needed. You can do this through fun events or lighthearted contests, for example. You may also want to plan for some "quick wins" that will build momentum early on.
4. **Make the Change "Stick":** Find ways to keep your initiative thriving and close to your most important stakeholders. Even if your change is implemented, be sure to reward behavior that aligns with the change through public praise or other forms of recognition. Make the initiative real to people by sharing stories of how the change has helped the company or benefited people.

5. **Operationalize the Change:** Once the change has been institution-alized, find ways to hold people accountable to the change. Account-ability may mean reeducating people or ensuring that recognition is given for reinforcement. As you continually solicit feedback on the change, be sure that you are showing people how change has been accomplished through quantifiable methods.

Make continuous improvement a way of life at your organization and do not be afraid to take a risk and lead a charge. The best change is one in which you have maximized a group's strengths to move the organization ahead. Similar to the concept of high performance teaming, in which the whole of a group is more than the sum of its parts, use your own abilities and those around you to create ideal outcomes. Once you engage in a change process such as this, you will notice that your political capital increases, which can make you a sought-after change-maker and doer.

SOCIAL NETWORK ANALYSIS

As you consider how to effect change with groups, you may want to look through the lens of social network analysis, a concept that has become increasingly popular in business and sociology. The major underpinning of social network analysis is that the ties that bind the human behavior of a group can provide helpful insights above individual behavior alone (International Network for Social Network Analysis [INSNA], 2008). How does this apply to the workplace? Some social networking theories hold that those people at the center of many relationships have even more influ-ence than people in high positions in the organization.

For example, if you were looking to make a culture change where peo-ple actually ate in the lunchroom at lunch time rather than in isolation at their desks, you might go to those with the most influence and at the cen-ter of the most relationships to get some momentum behind the change. By selecting these people to be part of your change effort, you will likely see a faster and more lasting change since you approached the most influ-ential people. Consider the questions below as you move forward with your change efforts:

- What kind of social networks exist at your organization? Who is at the center of these networks?
- When have you seen a change initiative be effective?
- Who was involved in making that change?
- What kind of support did it take to make the change?

- What kind of buy-in did it take to execute the change? From leaders? From employees?
- Who has contacts critical to the change required?
- Who could be impacted by the change you would like to make?

TRANSPARENT COMMUNICATION LESSENS NEGATIVE POLITICS

Open, honest communication is a great and long-lasting strategy for handling politics. If you think about it, it is hard to be seen as an honest, direct communicator and also be seen as someone who is highly political. Whether that means openly admitting mistakes, saying what you really think, or generally just being direct with people, transparent communication is probably the very best political tactic available to you.

One method for using transparent communication relates to how you manage successes or failures. Erin McGinnis shares, "My boss is great at managing politics—if he makes a mistake, he owns up to it immediately and is quick to make it right." When you work in an environment with a healthy tolerance for risk and mistakes, you can more easily own up to something that did not go as planned. Erin went on to recommend, "I think it helps to be perceptive of the culture and to be direct with people." Directness is something that we simply do not see enough of in business. Be the one to ask the tough questions and say what you really think. If you need to recalibrate this skill or tone it down, tell your boss that directness is a skill you are working on and that you would like his or her opinion if it is ever "too much."

Some minimize their involvement with politics by using strategies to prevent them, or by disengaging from them altogether. Roxanne Spillett, President and Chief Executive Officer of Boys and Girls Clubs of America, advised, "Just ignore politics. Staying above political dynamics is the best strategy I've seen." Similarly, Katharine Weymouth, Publisher of the *Washington Post* and Chief Executive Officer of Washington Post Media, shared, "While you're always going to be negotiating within a bureaucracy of some type, you don't want to get too involved in the politics. You need to play within it, but it helps to be very direct and ask people squarely, 'What do I need to do to get this done?'"

Jamie McCourt, President of the Los Angeles Dodgers, shared a slightly different approach, noting, "I don't have a lot of time for office politics. I find them very draining. To lessen politics, I go out of my way to keep everyone in my organization on the same page. I try to keep people bonded and aligned so that there is true strength in the team.

I always say, 'One plus one should equal more than two when it comes to team synergy.'" Jamie's point about open communication is astute. Being transparent and open is a great way to protect yourself and your team from misunderstandings or political blood baths. It also creates cohesion among a team that sets a precedent and expectation for straight talk.

Dominique Schurman, Chief Executive Officer of Papyrus, builds on this idea, "I think it helps when your company has an expectation that people should talk about facts and not just opinion, emotion, or innuendo. When everyone communicates this way, discussion is open and transparent. Keep things fact-based, not personal, and reward honest, open behavior in others. This style eliminates the room for noise." While emotions are a powerful tool for sensing what is going on in your company, they are not a good way to substantiate a point or speak with influence. Facts will always have far more sway than more emotive statements that start with "I feel" and "I sense." Lora J. Villarreal, Ph.D., Executive Vice President and Chief People Officer at Affiliated Computer Services, Inc. (ACS), talks about how we all have to train ourselves to think with a fact-based mentality, "I'm always straight with people. I never make assumptions, especially being in HR, I always look for facts and avoid depending on rumors. Rumors are like playing a game of telephone—by the time the remark gets back to the person it was said about—it's so distorted that you need to make it a habit to go by facts alone."

Communicating directly and honestly with people will win you more respect than buffering your remarks. For women, in particular, this can take adjusting to since there can be a fear of being harsh, damaging relationships or a worry that you will not be liked for your directness. Take a leap, even if you try to do so in a small way at first. Then build your "straight talk" successes up so that you can use them in any venue, with any audience.

WHEN YOU KNOW YOU'RE RIGHT

Speaking up and delivering the message when you are impassioned about something can be hard to do. For others, this trait is one they have to soften. Donna Callejon commented on the latter perspective, sharing, "Being respectfully candid is important. For me, it's been a lifetime of calibrating this quality so that I do it with the right people and use the right timing." Whether you think your organization is going in the wrong direction, a product is not going to be welcomed by your customers, or employees will not embrace a new initiative, there will always be situations where you disagree with the corporate direction.

So how do you know *how much* to voice your disagreement? Carla Lucchino notes, "I don't back down when I think I'm right. In the past, people have told me they respected me for holding my ground. I also care about ethics and keeping my reputation in tact. I do research to make sure that I'm the smartest person in the room . . . ." In Carla's case, if she feels she is right, that is grounds to push her idea forward. For Denise Incandela, however, there is a limit to how much she will protest an issue. Said Denise, "When there is an issue where I disagree with a colleague, or the direction my company is taking, I know when to back off. I have a rule that I am comfortable communicating my point of view three times and if I can't convince others to agree with me then I let the issue die." You may want to consider what your own limit is on what and how much you need to say to get your point across.

BUSINESS FOCUS AND RESULTS HELP TO DIFFUSE ISSUES

When in a difficult or contentious political situation, one of the best strategies you can use is to redirect the focus to the work that needs to get done. Denise Incandela told me, "I have . . . found that the best way to diffuse a political situation is to bring the challenge back to the business and away from people's personal bias. 'What's the best answer for the business?'" Asking this question during a heated meeting is likely to be a refreshing break from the charge and emotions in the room. It will also jolt people back to what is most important and pull them out of thinking only about interpersonal squabbles.

Katharine Weymouth furthers this idea sharing, "Nothing says 'take me seriously' like results. Demonstrating your ability to deliver will earn you respect." If you are mired in politics, go back to the area you can influence, which is your work. Rather than getting caught up in politicking, there are times when it is smartest to simply bring your focus back to delivering top-notch results. Agreeing with this idea, Melissa M. Monk, Chief Infrastructure Officer at Capital One, noted, "Delivering results can really give you a personal brand and an entrée to participate in things you otherwise couldn't. After that, it's about your ability to influence. Avoid making things personal by keeping your focus on the company, the customers, and [the] employees. Use value as your compass and you will never go wrong."

INTEGRITY AND ETHICS

It is important in office politics to recognize when an issue has crossed over into the realm of ethics. When politics bleed into an area where you need to question your ethics or the ethics of the organization, you will likely need to take some kind of action. DeeDee Wilson, Chief Financial Officer at Aritzia, shared, "I think it helps to be transparent with people and to know when and how to escalate issues up the ranks." Do not be afraid to approach someone more senior than you if an issue at work has raised an internal flag. If you do escalate an issue to management, always use facts, and not hearsay or opinion, to convey your point.

It is important to realize that integrity is an important trait needed to move into leadership. Executives, after all, manage millions of dollars and have many people's livelihoods at stake; so is it not critical that they be trustworthy? DeeDee Wilson also noted, "[S]taying true to your integrity and working hard to ensure those around you are successful is always the better way of dealing with things than relying on politics to get ahead." Therefore, the most helpful yardstick against which to measure your actions is your values. Consider what values are most important to you and hold yourself accountable to them.

TREATMENT OF OTHERS

Keep in mind that how you treat others says a lot about you. When you walk by the CEO of your company, do you say hello politely and yet ignore the mailroom clerk in a similar encounter? Part of mitigating negative politics is treating people equally and not blindly subscribing to others' assessments of people. D'Arcy Foster Rudnay warned against deciding on others' importance when she said, "[B]e respectful and kind to everyone—whether they are the chairman or the receptionist. You can't only be nice to important people." All of us have a certain amount of sway when it comes to our interactions with others. How you make people feel through your interactions says a lot about you.

TAKE INITIATIVE TO START
HEALTHY MOMENTUM

No matter what the personality of your organization, I recommend that you take some personal ownership in helping to create improvement. Rosslyn Kleeman shared some particularly inspirational words on this topic when she said, "Be outgoing, confident, and daring in your thinking. Even if there is no collegial atmosphere in a workplace, do it yourself and create one. It will make politics much easier to navigate." Rosslyn's advice to "do it yourself" is so right. It is up to you to create the kind of changes you want to see more of in your workplace. Strategies to keep in mind as you maneuver through politics include:

- End gossip by letting it die and wither with you. If you hear some news, even if it is compelling, do not take the next step of telling someone else.

- Be inclusive, particularly when in group settings. One way to do this is to speak openly to the group, avoiding side conversations, which tend to alienate others.
- Do not say anything verbally at work that you would not be comfortable saying over a loud speaker.
- Do not write anything at work that you would not be comfortable having published in a paper and attributed to you.
- Don't be afraid to go directly to a person to clarify an issue rather than letting the issue worsen or get increasingly distorted.
- Use fact-based communication when making a point, not emotion or innuendo. Use emotion to read situations but not to substantiate your point.
- If you disagree with where your organization is going, voice your concerns. If your concerns are repeatedly denied, you need to either get on board or leave.

Every workplace has a distinct personality. Human nature translates to ingrained dynamics, which we digest in the form of cues, body language, and treatment. Successfully navigating politics will help you work in the most collegial of atmospheres, or can help in more politically charged environments where you will need to "swim with the sharks without becoming one."

Mastering the Work/Life Seesaw

HAVING IT ALL

Chances are, you want to pursue a lot—an exciting career, time for your loved ones, and space to develop personally. Many members of Generations X and Y have grown up with the message that women *can* have it all. After all, these generations most likely saw their mothers juggling areas like work and philanthropy, in addition to the care of children, parents, and other loved ones—all while attempting to fit in their own health and well-being. This chapter examines the concept of work/life balance throughout the lifecycle of one's career. Self-care, including how to manage your time in the short-term and long-term, is also discussed.

THE CURRENT STATE OF EXTREME WORK

Given the current day of blackberries, beepers, and connectedness to the office, the "extreme job" has emerged as a common reality for many leaders and aspiring leaders. Sylvia Ann Hewlett, President and Founder of the Center for Work-Life Policy, has conducted pioneering research on the topic. Hewlett's study showed that 21 percent of the high earners she surveyed held extreme jobs, meaning that they logged 60 or more hours a week at work, and only one-fifth of them were women. According to Hewlett, extreme jobs have implications that mean more women are losing out (Hewlett & Luce, 2006). Hewlett noted,

> Women pay a disproportionate price for their extreme jobs and are being left behind in new ways. Over the past 40 years, highly credentialed women flooded into the professional labor market and, at least

in some sectors, started to make serious progress—rising up the ranks, snapping at the heels of men. Then high-level jobs were redefined. They became even more time consuming, even more pressure filled—increasingly beyond the reach of women with significant childcare and eldercare responsibilities. The result: Only 20 percent of extreme job holders are female, and fully 80 percent of them have one foot out the door because they feel they can't keep up a 70-hour week for more than 12 months. (Hewlett & Luce, 2007)

Shifts toward extreme work do not appear to be lessening, particularly given the current environment of corporate downsizing, in which one person can be expected to do jobs that two people formerly held. Extreme jobs are common at the top of organizations and, therefore, it is more important than ever that women are fairly represented in the leadership of companies, in part, so this dynamic can be changed. Even though women make up roughly half of the workforce, the corporate structures and policies in U.S. workplaces do not yet reflect the needs of both male and female employees. The case for employers accommodating those who provide care for dependents is significant. Why? For one, it is no longer women alone who are charged with caring for aging parents, children, and other loved ones with disabilities. While women have and continue to shoulder the majority of this care, it is in employers' best favor to create an environment inclusive of the whole workforce. Additionally, if employers want to retain their female workforce, they will need to take more supportive actions to embrace this group rather than just increase the demands on them.

THE "YOU CAN HAVE IT ALL" MESSAGE

The message that women can "have it all" can be at the same time liberating and quite overwhelming. The image conjured up of today's "Superwoman" is made up of a cast of conflicting characters; a hard-nosed executive that is admired and respected at work, a loving and doting mother that never misses a single school play, a wife that keeps the romance alive with her partner, maintaining her femininity and physical attractiveness, all while Superwoman develops her spiritual side and makes time for girlfriends and hobbies. Dizzying, is it not? Do not get me wrong, it is truly wonderful to have progressed to a point where women make up roughly half of the workforce and have untold opportunities available to them that they did not in the recent past. However, the expectations of women as heads of households have not evolved very much to account for the increased pressure in other parts of life, such as work. Instead, many women feel they are expected to do it all, and do it well. This makes for a pressure-filled dynamic in which women are now expected to be ambitious professionals in addition to leading their outside lives with just as much devotion, commitment, and energy.

In the case of Shannon S. S. Herzfeld, Vice President of Government Relations at Archer Daniels Midland Company, she was able to strike a comfortable equilibrium in the areas of her life. She recalled, "I wouldn't have believed earlier in my career that I'd be 56 years old and successful in all parts of my life. I am a strong, competent business leader and also a caring and loving mother and wife. I always wanted to grow daughters that felt that the world was wide open to them, and I think I accomplished that." As Shannon points out, "having it all" is certainly dependent on what success and happiness mean to you.

While I encourage you to give your energy to the areas of life that excite you most, what do you do if there are simply too many commitments to which you can give? For one, striving to satisfy all areas of your life equally is not a realistic goal. Rather, as many of the established career women I interviewed noted, sacrifice is a daily reality. Dominique Schurman, Chief Executive Officer of Papyrus, reflected, "The tensions between work and personal areas of your life are real. I'm not sure that we talk about that enough. There's a doctrine out there that women can have it all, and while that's a wonderful message, it's not that simple. We owe young women the full truth. Your lifestyle is about your values, and women can pursue it all, but there are sacrifices involved." Dominique aptly encapsulates the Superwoman phenomenon, including the fact that there are both negative and positive aspects to it. Similarly, Vicki Ho, General Manager, Asia Services for GE Healthcare Clinical Services at General Electric, shared, "It's no badge of glory for me to say that I've missed loved one's birthdays . . . but ultimately each person needs to find their own right balance."

Dominique Schurman added a great piece of advice on finding contentment and satisfaction: to make sure that our values are nurtured and fed. When you are unclear on what your values are, it is much more difficult to seek out and live a life that is fulfilling. When you do have knowledge of your values, you have a guiding compass that can tell you when you have drifted off course or that confirms you are on the right path. Consider what your most deeply held values are and allow your life's decisions to emanate from them.

WORK/LIFE INTEGRATION

Since perfect balance between the areas of your life is extremely difficult to achieve—and may not even be what you want—I suggest you seek out a different goal. Following the advice of the leaders I interviewed, I recommend you strive instead to *integrate* your work/life priorities, calibrating them as your passions and interest dictate. When I asked Barbara A. F. Greene, Chief Executive Officer of Greene and Associates, Inc., for an example of how she makes time for herself, she responded candidly, "It's not a piece of cake. I don't really think of it in terms of work/life balance, I think in terms of integrating all of the things that are meaningful to me." Similarly, Jamie McCourt, President of the Los Angeles Dodgers, shared, "I don't believe there is such a thing as work/life balance. Our focus will usually go where it's needed most at the time, and that's a target that is always going to change. Sometimes the focus might be a husband, kids, philanthropy, teaching, or work." The concept of work/life integration deviates from our usual thinking of work/life balance in that balance conveys striking an even distribution between work and personal worlds. This is very hard to achieve for many individuals, and in many cases is not what brings people the biggest sense of satisfaction.

Work/life integration, on the other hand, provides a new paradigm that implies giving energy to different areas of your life, and carefully calibrating your energy based on your strongest values and priorities at the time. As an example, one woman may enjoy a job that pushes her to her limits, provided she has ample time to work out on the weekends and evenings. Another woman may enjoy the flexibility she gets from working a 30-hour-per-week job, because it affords her time to volunteer at her favorite cause. Yet another woman may appreciate her ability to stay home with her young children so that she can play a major role in their young lives, while also having time to be involved in committees at their school. Integration is all about understanding what is important to you now, and building a life that allows you to interlace it all into your schedule.

Kelly Pickett, a senior manager at a management consulting firm, supported this sentiment noting, "The funny thing about work/life balance is that just when you get it right—with your kids for example—something changes and you need to recalibrate the whole plan." Finding ways to multitask the different areas of your life is an ongoing job, many times composed of moving targets and priorities.

HOW DOES INTEGRATION LOOK FOR YOU?

How integration actually "looks" differs for everyone. I encourage you to do the following exercise as a way to see where you are putting your energy and where you might like to change your focus (see Figure 8.1). To get a sense of what is most important to you, segment sections of the circle on the left so that it is separated into the ideal themes of your life. After sectioning a theme off, label each theme. You might use labels such as: Work, Family, Home Management, Health & Wellness, Spirituality, Socializing, Care of Others, Fun, and Commuting. The size of the "pie slice" indicates

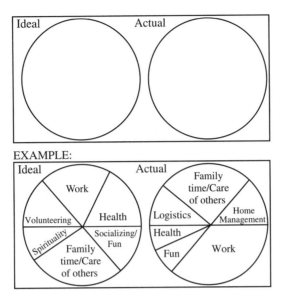

Figure 8-1. Life Themes—Ideal versus Actual

how prominent you would like that theme to be in your life. Once you have completed categorizing how you want to spend your time, use the circle on the right to plot out how your current life actually breaks down.

Are the results the same? For most of us, the answer is "no." However, this powerful but simple exercise can quickly wake us up from our haze and help us to see our current reality in terms of how we spend our days. This is an exercise that I recommend you do throughout your life; I especially like this exercise for the clarity it brings. A journal or diary can be an ideal place to record this kind of exercise and any related thoughts. Looking at your ideal versus actual themes tends to cut through any ambiguity and get right to the heart of your time investments. Once you fill in both circles, you can then analyze the gap to see where there are areas that are taking up too much or too little time—or those areas that are important to you but did not even make it into your circle!

WHAT DOES IT REALLY TAKE TO LEAD?

No matter how you choose to divide your energies, the women I interviewed stressed that leadership requires a certain level of "toughness"—also known as "stamina." Given the kinds of decisions that executives must make every day, mental, emotional, intellectual, and physical stamina are necessities. Those in leadership are required to decide if a layoff is necessary, if a merger or acquisition is a risk worth taking, if a new product is worth investing in, and what the strategic direction of the organization should be. Executives are also frequently called upon to work long hours and travel on short notice for work. Sharing this information is by no means intended to scare you out of leadership; quite the opposite in fact. By looking at the demands of most leadership jobs square in the face, it can help young women to decide if the kind of lifestyle experienced by many women executives is appealing and functional for them. Also, just because executive level jobs have been comprised one way in the past, does not mean they will need to look exactly the same in the future.

Said Roxanne Spillett, President and Chief Executive Officer of Boys and Girls Clubs of America, "Physical and mental stamina have helped me be successful. Fortunately, I have good genes for that." Mental toughness is an absolute requirement for senior management, a job that does not always fit neatly into an 8-hour day. The nature of travel, long hours, and spontaneous crises translate into leaders needing a true capacity for hard work. Leadership also requires the ability to focus, crowding out personal or other distractions. You can start to identify your level of mental stamina by asking your boss and others around you how well you work and focus during times of pressure. You can also take the time to observe how you handle stress on the job. You most likely engage in activities currently that are developing your mental discipline; look for opportunities to do more of them.

Staying organized can also be a major help in staying mentally sharp and on-task. When your work tasks are organized into some kind of system with clear priorities, you can surely be more productive. I remember seeing a Larry King interview with Martha Stewart in which the topic of her legendary success came up. Martha said, "People always ask me, how do you get so much done? . . . It is because I am . . . more organized than other people" (CNN, 2001). How interesting that a woman who owns a major, successful media outfit attributes her success most to staying organized!

Emotional stamina plays yet another role in a leader keeping herself mentally tough. The women I interviewed cited the characteristic of unflappability as being particularly important as a woman leader. While you will want to use your emotional savvy to read people, circumstances, and situations, I recommend that you choose wisely which times to put your emotional reactions on display for all to see. When I asked Dominique Schurman what piece of advice stayed with her most over the years, she responded, "Keep an even keel. Never let them see you sweat. . . . Be positive and steady." She went on to share, "A leader can't wear their feelings on their sleeve. Especially as a woman, you simply can't show too much vulnerability because people are watching you carefully." Remaining emotionally tough is a challenge when work touches and affects us in emotional ways. Whether it is a problem employee that aggravates you to no end, a project from hell that seems to have sucked away your happiness, or a public mistake that you made, picking yourself back up and projecting an air of confidence is vitally important.

Your physical stamina may certainly be tested during periods of long hours, excessive travel, or when the rest of your life is exhausting you to the point that you do not have sufficient energy. Denise Incandela, President of Saks Direct at Saks Fifth Avenue, recalled, "I used to work 16 hours a day, but now that I have a two year old I have pared it back to 11 hours a day. Now that I have a daughter, I try to be more efficient, delegate more often, and work smarter. Doing this makes me feel good about my work/life balance." For Denise, she has thoughtfully managed where she puts her time and energy and has had success with it. Excessive hours are an expectation of executives in many types of business. In certain organizations, people who work long hours are rewarded for it, since it is seen as an extension of one's commitment and dedication. Roxanne Spillett noted, "Being a really hard worker has helped me be taken seriously. I am known around the office for working 6 a.m. to 9 p.m. days."

One proven outlet for helping to sharpen mental focus, release stress, and improve physical toughness is exercise. Numerous interviewees credited some form of exercise in helping them to be more successful at work. DeeDee Wilson, Chief Financial Officer at Aritzia, encouraged women to find a release, advising, "Find time to recharge. Whether it's exercise, yoga, travel, or something else you love, find activities that give you a break from work, allow you to center yourself, and come back refreshed." The benefits of exercise are numerous, and I cannot stress enough the positive domino effect that exercise can have on your life. Aerobic exercise can boost your self-confidence and respect for your body, areas where women can always use more quantity.

Setting aside time to meet your own needs is an important part of self-care. Autumn Bayles, Senior Vice President of Strategic Operations at Tasty Baking Company, noted, "[I approach work/life balance] judiciously. . . . You have to set limits on your commitments. For me, I try to make time to work out every day, which is time just for me." Time alone, or designated to your own self-care, can replenish you in untold ways. What physical activity can you do to support your performance at work and in the rest of your life? Do you eat healthfully? Do you sleep enough? Each of these areas has an affect on what kind of contribution you will bring to work.

USING YOUR SUPPORT SYSTEM

Nourishing your career aspirations requires that you tap fully into your support system. Many women I interviewed conveyed that they did not make it to the top without help from others, crediting the importance of the love, support, and encouragement of their friends and family. Melissa M. Monk, Chief Infrastructure Officer at Capital One, noted, "It's all about knowing what's important to you. When I decided to go back to school, for example, I knew I needed to talk to those who were close to me about my priorities, being clear about what I could and couldn't do, and delivering on what I said I would. I've had to say explicitly when my focus was only on work, only on school, or only on home. I think many people forget to talk to those close to them about priorities." Communicating with your support system is critical. Even if you are tempted to try to "go it alone," reaching out—and if nothing else, sharing your current situation—will help you to get the feedback, encouragement, or support you need.

Erin McGinnis, National Committee Chair of the Society of Women Engineers, takes this notion a step further, advising, "You need to have the courage to ask for what you need in life—finding support in peers, your manager, or people outside of work. These people are around so that you can bounce your ideas off of them. You need to ask for what you want without feeling guilty about it." Asking for what you want and need from others is so extremely critical for women. While many women are conditioned to accommodate others before putting their own interests forward, do not be afraid to ask those around you for what you want and need.

NEGOTIATING FOR NONTRADITIONAL WORK ARRANGEMENTS

One area where women can make strides to improve the workplace for all is in negotiating for nontraditional work arrangements. Even if there is resistance at your organization to offering flexible or part-time working arrangements, do not let that stop you from asking for what you need. Furthermore, research shows that these arrangements do not lead to decreased productivity as many business leaders fear. An MIT Sloan School of Management study, for example, suggests that job flexibility can offer many benefits to both employers and employees, including improved job satisfaction, reduced absenteeism, greater commitment, and reduced turnover (Bailyn, Drago, & Kochan, 2001).

Also showing positive support for flexible work arrangements, a Boston College Center for Work & Family study of six large companies showed that 70 percent of managers and 87 percent of employees reported that a flexible arrangement had a positive or very positive impact on productivity; 65 percent of managers and 87 percent of employees reported that a flexible work arrangement had a positive or very positive impact on the quality of work; and 76 percent of managers and 80 percent of employees indicated that flexible work arrangements had positive effects on retention (Pruchno, Litchfield, & Fried, 2000). Companies that ignore the makeup and needs of their total workforce are making a major mistake, as their unaccommodated employees will leave and go elsewhere.

Many women seek a different kind of work arrangement from traditional hours, whether in the form of job sharing, reduced work hours, telecommuting, or another creative configuration. If you are in a situation where you would like to make a request for a new arrangement, first collect relevant background information. With a request to become a full-time telecommuter, for example, the first thing I would recommend you do is to estimate how much time you actually spend in the office and how much your duties require you to be physically present at work. If it is clear that your work can be done relatively easily at home, be prepared to make a case, complete with all the facts that explain how a new arrangement would work.

If you are looking for a job, I encourage you to seek out those organizations that support people in terms of flexible work arrangements and work/life integration. Many such companies have been recognized in publicized ranked lists such as the annual Working Mother 100 Best Companies list by *Working Mother* magazine or *Fortune* magazine's 100 Best Companies to Work For® in America list. Melissa Monk noted, "I think everyone—men and women—feel a pressure to say 'yes' when they're new to the work world and low in confidence. For women specifically, I think it helps to work at a company like mine that supports people's changes in their lives. We have all kinds of flexible work arrangements to accommodate and retain working moms, for example. We recognize the value of our people and value diversity." Purposefully seeking out a company that is flexible toward employees' needs and life changes is important. You can research companies with a reputation for flexibility, ask your network which companies have good work/life practices, and ask directly about an organization's approach in an interview.

THE MOTHERHOOD PREDICAMENT

Women's careers can have a way of blossoming at the same time that they want to have children. Surely, this can present a predicament if the expectation put on us (whether external or self-imposed) is that there is one "best" time to focus on either career or family. Erin McGinnis commented on the topic noting, "The biggest challenge women face is the high expectations people have of them in all aspects of their lives. People expect women to be successful in the same ways men are at work, to be traditionally good mothers, and to take care of all the other loose ends in life—from getting your dry cleaning—to trying to stay healthy—to preparing

food every night. All of these commitments take time and happen throughout our entire lives. There is really no ideal time to focus on your career."
Many interviewees noted a similar sentiment; the only *perfect* time for
having a family or investing heavily in your career is the time that you
decide is right.

Contrary to the pervading belief of many women, raising a family does
not necessarily translate to losing or bruising one's career. That said,
research paints a bleak picture of women's historical experiences leaving
the workplace. A study, entitled *BACK IN THE GAME: Returning to Business after a Hiatus,* conducted by the Wharton Center for Leadership and
Change and the Forté Foundation, analyzed perceptions of women reentering the workforce after leaving to raise a family, care for a parent, or
address other personal matters. The study showed that 70% of women
surveyed felt positive about leaving their full-time jobs at first, only to
have their optimism significantly decrease as they attempted reentry into
the workplace later. Many women found the experience to be negative
and expressed frustration or depression when faced with their job search.
The study also uncovered that 83% of women either took a comparable
or lower role than the one they held before their hiatus. A meager 17% of
women reentered the workforce at a higher level than the one they held
before their hiatus. Interestingly, the study showed that most women who
went back to work tended to take positions with smaller companies or
they ultimately changed industries altogether (McGrath, Driscoll, &
Gross, 2005). This survey quantifies, in a sobering way, the negative perceptions of women attempting to leave and then reintegrate into the
workplace.

When I asked Katherine Weymouth, Publisher of the *Washington Post*
and Chief Executive Officer of Washington Post Media, "Can women do
it all?" she replied candidly, "Kids add an additional complication to
women's work/life balance; the answer is 'no, we can't.'" The twin peaks
of career and children are complicated further by the fact that the
United States has one of the worst maternity leave policies in the world.
The United States is among five countries in the world that does not
require employers to offer employees a form of paid maternity leave.
According to a study by McGill University's Institute for Health and
Social Policy, the United States, Lesotho, Liberia, Papua New Guinea,
and Swaziland were the only countries out of 173 assessed that did not
guarantee any paid leave for mothers. Most of the countries studied
offer mothers 14 or more weeks of paid leave (Heymann, Earle, &
Hayes, 2007). Since the Family and Medical Leave Act was passed in
1993, U.S. workers are allowed to take up to 12 weeks leave to tend to
family or medical needs, but their absence is unpaid (U.S. Department

of Labor, 1993). Furthermore, in some states, women utilize short-term disability to receive partial pay during their maternity leave. What kind of message does it send that maternity leave is treated as a disability? With weaker policies than much of the world, American women face resistance, structurally and logistically, to their basic needs. Given such outdated aspects of the U.S. work culture, you need to rally all the more for what you need and deserve.

The process of taking maternity or other types of leave, therefore, requires thoughtful planning, just as you would prepare for any other important event in your personal or professional life. Carefully planning for your transition—both out of and back into—the workplace will pay dividends in many ways. For one, by creating a detailed "leave" plan as well as a "reentry" plan, you can help set expectations early on with your boss. Certainly those expectations can vary. Some women want to send the message, "I will be back and do not want you to give my job away." Other women wish to convey, "I plan to stay connected and will be in touch while I am on leave." Still other women would like to suggest, "My schedule will be less flexible when I return." Planning upfront shows that you care about the work that must be done in your absence and you feel a sense of ownership over your role. I suggest that you include in your leave and reentry plans key dates, tasks, and people. The study, *BACK IN THE GAME: Returning to Business after a Hiatus* specifically recommends that women create reentry plans that are "strategic and thoughtful, with specific and measurable goals" (McGrath, Driscoll, & Gross, 2005).

It can also be helpful to create your own personal version of a leave plan that includes your support network, as well as plans for childcare and time for your own self-care. Cynthia Egan, President of Retirement Plan Services at T. Rowe Price, advised, "Managing work and life is a big and complicated job. You need to create the infrastructure to support your personal life the way you would plan for the infrastructure of an organization. It helps to get in a rhythm and have top-notch childcare so that you are not worried about how your kids are doing." If you are fortunate enough to plan for and procure good-quality childcare, you can be that much more engaged, focused, and undistracted at work.

Once you are on leave, I recommend creating a network that helps you to feel supported and engaged. Whether that group is made up of other caregivers and parents, professionals, friends, family, or elders who have been through it all, do not try to navigate such a major life change on your own. This support network can serve to normalize your experiences and give you valuable feedback and advice during your life's milestones and transition periods.

STAYING CURRENT

Even if your maternity leave is technically a break from work, some women I interviewed noted that they chose not to sever all connections to the work world during their leave period. Courteney Monroe, Executive Vice President of Consumer Marketing at HBO, shared, "I am extremely lucky to have a supportive husband, wonderful childcare, and healthy kids. One choice I made was not to disconnect totally from the office when I went on two maternity leaves. I didn't want to be put on the 'mommy track.'" Courteney's point about the "mommy track" sheds light on the common work experience of women who have children, and return to the workplace only to find that motherhood has disqualified them for advancement. Staying connected, in some way or another, is a good way to keep current and aware of what is going on at the office. You can do this by attending a few critical meetings, or perhaps keeping up your relationships by seeing colleagues occasionally.

Some women I interviewed who took extended leaves have also found it helpful to take a formal volunteer role, join a membership organization, continue their education, or attend industry conferences. Any ways that you can keep your skills up-to-date and stay current on developments in your field and company will help you to remain competitive upon returning to work from a leave. Rosslyn Kleeman, Chair of the Coalition for Effective Change, reflected on this subject, noting, "Different skills have come in handy at different times in my life. The skills I found I needed most were when I came back to work after having four kids. You lose a lot of confidence when you're home with kids, so I needed to come back to work and quickly adapt to changing technology, office culture, and the work world." Some women have even found value in using this time to expand their network or breadth of work experiences. Volunteer positions with a business focus, paid positions that are part-time, or temporary work assignments can also help in this regard. Certainly projects, people, and work tasks forge ahead while you are gone. That is why the more you can follow a reentry plan and show your boss the results, the more squarely you can reposition yourself at work.

LIFE AFTER MATERNITY LEAVE— THE 80 PERCENT SOLUTION

So what actually happens after maternity leave? In the case of Courteney Monroe, her ability to give to all areas of her life certainly changed. Courteney shared, "It's pretty hard to balance work and life when you're a Type A control freak like me who is accustomed to giving 150%. I think I've gotten comfortable with the 80 percent solution—that's how much I'm able to give to each area of my life." Unfortunately, the process of returning to the workplace after taking leave goes largely ignored by businesses. In the United States, most men and women are not well supported by employers when it comes to taking time out for life transitions or reintegrating back into the workforce. That leaves much of the onus on the person returning to work to adjust, adapt, and find a routine that works for him or her. In Courteney's case, her ability to "have it all" means that she feels that she can only give 80% of herself to the different areas of her life. For many women I interviewed, the "80 Percent Solution" is a way to participate in many areas that are meaningful to you, even if you cannot give each of those areas your full, undivided attention and focus.

Some women I interviewed shared one particularly helpful part of a reentry plan. They maintained a support network after they had children and returned to work. That allowed for the exchange of ideas, encouragement, and discussion, and gave them a helpful logistical edge. Illustrating this, Cynthia Egan shared, "For me, a critical component of success at work has had to do with knowing that my kids were in good shape. By making good decisions about childcare and getting the right support, I've been able to bring my whole self to work." Another leader and mom, Rosslyn Kleeman, explained, "After having four kids, I went back to work but was lucky enough to be able to afford a housekeeper. This really helped. I realize that many people don't have that same luxury. Another thing that helped me was that when I left work to have my kids, I never totally disconnected myself from intellectual activities like chairing a board for public television or acting as the chair for the Council for the Gifted."

As part of many of the women's support networks, they recruited members of their inner circle to be among their backup help if they had a sick child or required other early school pick-ups. Giving yourself a contingency plan can help you to feel that you are not the only qualified person who can be called upon in emergencies. Giving yourself a backup plan also frees you up to better focus on and achieve more at work and helps you to feel more secure with regard to spontaneous, unforeseen events.

Another strategy for successfully reentering the workforce is to adopt a give-and-take approach. If you are able to clearly carve out boundaries around what you can and cannot do, then you can make the most of the time and energy that you can commit. Kelly Pickett said, "I heard once that it's all about integration rather than balance. I'm not great at compartmentalizing the different areas of my life; I'm more of a multitasker. I carry a yellow pad with me whenever I work in the office so that I can jot down a note or to-do that I may have forgotten. I try to prewire as much flexibility into my life as possible. What's worked best for me is to be very definitive with my limits and very flexible with my free time." Showing your boss that you have clear limits, but are flexible within the office hours you work, will help you to convey your willingness to be a team player.

THANK GOODNESS FOR FAMILY AND FRIENDS

Finding support from one's family and friends, particularly a partner or spouse, is critical to career success. Numerous women echoed this sentiment in their interviews. One example is Cathy Fleming, Partner at Nixon Peabody LLP, who reflected, "I always tried to put my kids first, and my job was a close second. Some times the order of those two switched but I really tried to prioritize my family. I think I was a better mom because I was happy at work. I also have a terrific, supportive spouse and the benefit of great relationships with my kids. . . ." While priorities may change throughout your life, having a caring spouse can certainly help you feel that you have a solid source of support in your life. Rosslyn Kleeman also credited her support system in helping her achieve success, noting, "My loved ones have been very important in encouraging me and helping me be my best at work. My parents gave me lots of confidence and my father encouraged my love of politics, even though it wasn't work that was considered appropriate for women. My husband also supported my career and my success."

When DeeDee Wilson and I discussed this topic, she relayed, "I read a statistic once that said that 80 percent of male leaders have partners that stay at home, while only 20 percent of women leaders do. I think women underestimate the amount of energy it takes to be both a leader in business and a leader in the home. In my case, my husband and I decided I would be the primary breadwinner and that he would stay home with our daughter. This has worked out beautifully for us. He tells people that 'We earn DeeDee's salary'—and he is so right. I could never have advanced in my career without his support." Support of your closest loved ones can take many forms. A spouse's emotional support, flexibility, and interest in sharing child rearing responsibilities can make all the difference as you navigate your career.

Just as DeeDee and others have done, I encourage you to find a way to ask for what you want and need from those closest to you. Your choices, such as your choice of partner, will certainly have an impact on how high you climb at work and how good you feel about doing so. Patricia Deyton, Director of the Center for Gender in Organizations at Simmons School of Management, advised, "Moving up in the work world requires a huge commitment and yet the same level of commitment, if not more, is required when you have a family. The workplace tends to demand that work comes first and this is incompatible with managing a family. You need to have the kind of personal life that supports you doing both things and you really need to choose your partner carefully." If you are career-minded and interested in leading, look for a partner that has the capacity for caring and support. A supportive spouse is invaluable as you are tested emotionally, physically, and intellectually; the beauty of a supportive partnership is that you can help and encourage each other throughout your careers.

When seeking integration between your work and personal lives, trust that you can find an equilibrium that is right for you. You may learn through trial and error what works and what does not, but know that you can find a workable solution. I would encourage you to think in terms of possibilities rather than limits. Furthermore, if others put limits on you or discourage you, consider the advice but do not necessarily take it! As Shannon Herzfeld noted, "The most important advice I heard was the advice that I didn't take. That advice was that you couldn't have a man's job or travel because you had children. There was a lot of gender-specific advice I chose not to take."

SUCCEEDING ON THE JOB MEANS YOU NEED A LIFE!

One of the most overlooked keys to succeeding on the job is ensuring that you have a fulfilling life outside of work. As intuitive as this concept seems, it is easy for highly ambitious and motivated women to forget. Cultivating a full life outside of your work will sustain you, allow you to come back to work refreshed, and many times it will make you even more effective at work. Additionally, being a well-rounded person brings a measure of depth, satisfaction, and balance to your work. Catherine J. Mathis, Senior Vice President of Corporate Communications at The New York Times Company, told me, "My life is out of balance and I like it that way. There are times when work can be too much, but there are techniques for managing it. All of us need to take time off, go on vacations, and get refreshed." I encourage you to use your vacation time, disconnect completely, and come back refreshed and renewed. Many Americans forget that vacation time is a benefit meant for using!

Jamie McCourt shared with me, "I try to take part in things that help me to feel grounded. I make time to swim every day, which is something I do just for me. I also really love to cook and do that out of necessity and for enjoyment." Partaking in nourishing activities will always give back to you in several ways. Moreover, having a wide breadth of personal experiences translates to a win-win situation for you and your employer.

WORK CREEP

When you do not attend to your priorities or monitor how much attention they are getting, you risk losing your sense of equilibrium. Roxanne Spillett recalled, "Looking back, what really creeps up on you is that your job can consume your life. Jobs like the one I have *become* your life and I wish I had left more time for a normal balance. If you're going to lead, you need to figure out for yourself what kind of work/life balance you require." Similarly, when I asked Dominique Schurman about work/life balance, she explained, "It's very hard and one of the biggest challenges for women. I've found that my career can be all-encompassing; thoughts of work are never far away. Even though I enjoy my personal life, it's hard to put work on the shelf."

Your career, particularly when it is challenging and fulfilling, can have a way of seeping into your outside life. When I asked Carla E. Lucchino, Assistant Deputy Commandant, Installations and Logistics at the U.S. Marine Corps, "How do you integrate work and life?" she candidly shared, "I'm not that good at it. You need a spouse or positive magnet to pull you away from work and make you want to draw a line between work and personal life. I'm divorced without kids and some would say that's a byproduct of being a career-driven woman." Patricia Deyton also commented on the importance of having people and things outside of work that pull you away from the job. She told me, "There are tradeoffs. I was better at balancing my life when I had a young family; but now that I have more time to dedicate to work, it's harder to draw a line between work and home. I think a lot of it is about choice—I am choosing to engage in a lot of things right now that interest me."

One simple way to keep an eye on this is to monitor your level of engagement and passion, along with the actual hours you are working. Many companies use timekeeping systems and ask employees to fill in timesheets. If your organization does not have such a system, keep your own log of hours to watch how much you are working and the status of your overall well-being. The challenges of being a high-powered professional will always be there for women who play multiple roles. By taking an integrated approach to life, you can get the most fulfillment and enjoyment out of it, and at the same time demonstrate attention and care for yourself.

IT'S OKAY TO SAY NO SOMETIMES

Can an aspiring leader say "no" to work assignments and still move up at work? The answer is "yes"—if you choose your "no's" carefully. DeeDee Wilson emphasized,

Generations X and Y look at work/life balance differently, and because of that it's more acceptable these days to say 'no' to international projects or assignments with travel. If you do say 'no,' make sure your argument is well thought out, not emotional, and that you provide alternatives. Don't say 'no' all the time. In my career, being willing to travel, to do things outside the norm, and to even be willing to live outside the USA have helped me progress— not just because I said 'yes' to the opportunities, but because I learned so much in those circumstances that I was better able to grow and add value.

Certainly, saying "no" is needed if you are overloaded beyond your capacity to do quality work. In those cases, give your boss compelling, rational reasons why you need to decline the opportunity. I recommend coming up with alternatives if and when you say "no." One way of expressing this is to say something like, "I would love to be part of the internal taskforce you suggested, but given the demands of the Johnson and Myer accounts, I would need one of those clients to come off my plate before I could serve on the taskforce." Phrasing an alternative, or a condition to you taking on a task, shows your boss that you want to do a good job but that your resources are not unlimited. Erin McGinnis encourages, "[Y]ou need a good reason [to say 'no']. If you say you can't stay late, give a reason and be upfront. I think it's important that if you have to say 'I can't make it work this time' that you can counter that by offering another time when you can do it. Ask the question, 'Can we create a way for me to still do this?'"

MEANING AND FULFILLMENT LEADS TO BALANCE

Charles R. Stoner and Jennifer Robin, coauthors of the book *A Life in Balance: Finding Meaning in a Chaotic World,* conducted some eye-opening research on work/life balance. Their research, based on interviews with leaders across the country, shows that work/life balance is not as dependent on time management skills as you think. Robin explained, "Our premise is that time management/life management really doesn't solve the balance issue. The reason is that balance isn't about time, it is about meaning. That means it is flexible, changeable, and needs to be viewed holistically" (2009). The research of Stoner and Robin reiterates that finding harmony is a moving target.

Robin went on to share the following recommendation for women looking to balance their lives:

Determine your anchors (career, health, family, spirituality, etc.) and the basic needs of each. Once those are determined, the rest of your time and energy should be spent on activities that bring your life meaning, or a sense of well-being. Those activities are often ones where you get to use your unique strengths. We also suggest that it is a process of trial and error, and being open to learning as you go. Even a 'failure' is a chance to learn about what meaning 'means' for you. The biggest danger in the process is going in believing that you must have the perfect solution to balance your life. (Robin, 2009)

At the heart of authentic leadership is knowing that your life and its parts have significance and worth. Illustrating this point, Denise Incandela told me, "I feel very balanced. I love what I do, so for me to be at work is a pleasure." You are the only one who can decide if your life is congruent with your deepest held values. How much meaning does your life have?

AVOIDING BURNOUT

If you are saddled with demands, it is important that you be vigilant for signs of burnout. Burnout is the feeling of depletion—mentally, physically, intellectually, emotionally—that leads to a feeling of disillusionment or disengagement. Most of us know someone who has experienced prolonged stress and consequently was burned out for some period of their lives. Burnout can hurt your performance at work and lessen your ability to be fully present and engaged in the other areas of life. Whether burnout is caused by self-imposed or outside demands, it is a real consequence of "overworking." Maya Rockeymoore, Ph.D., President and Founder of Global Policy Solutions, recommended, "You have to be cognizant of your choices. I've made the mistake of focusing only on my work and that left me burned out at the age of 29. Professional success is empty without personal rewards, like friendships and strong relationships. Sometimes I've had to turn down great opportunities if it meant I couldn't strike the right work/life balance."

To avoid burnout, consider keeping a diary that chronicles when and where your stress is heightened. Doing this will surface patterns in your work that trigger the most stress for you. I would also encourage you to note the opposite effect. Be vigilant of when and where you feel energized, motivated, and excited in your workday. If you feel that burnout is imminent, consider taking some time off right away to recharge. Alternatively, look for opportunities to do more of what energizes you and less of what drains you. Remember, if you are feeling burned out, chances are you cannot afford to do nothing. Ask yourself these questions as you understand your own relationship to burnout:

- What drains my energy? What tasks do I dread?
- What feeds my energy? What tasks do I look forward to?

- What support or resources are available to me? Emotionally? Physically?
- Where can I delegate some tasks?
- What am I doing for my own self-care and development?
- What can I do to renew myself in the short term? In the long term?
- What areas of my life are more vulnerable and which parts are more resilient?
- What can I do to feel more centered? What are one small thing and one big thing that I can do to feel better?
- How can I better fulfill my immediate needs?

Considering these questions will help you as you understand both what energizes you and what drains you, and if you can do something more about it. Melissa Monk recommended, "Know what you love to do and the rest will follow. Find out what kind of culture you like, what gives you energy, and focus on that." If you are in a dysfunctional, negative, or toxic environment, I strongly encourage you to consider leaving. Certainly one cause of burnout and an indicator that you could be in the wrong job or field is an overall lack of fulfillment. If you are lacking a "Plan B" for your next job or career move, take the time to consider what excites you and what limits you using the questions above. You should take the time to contemplate why you went into your current line of work and if you experience a match between your personal values and the values upheld in your job.

THINKING SHORT- AND LONG-TERM

Planning and implementing work/life integration is something you can do in both short- and long-term ways. Clearly, in the short term, you can plan for the details of your day-to-day life, including how you will spend your time and where you will designate your energy. Jeanine Becker, Senior Counsel at Motorola, Inc., however, views her career in a forward-looking way, noting, "I don't see work/life balance in a short-term 'day' or 'week' kind of way. I see it over years. We all have different priorities at different times in our lives. Right out of school, I certainly worked more hours. Now I work from home a lot and want a different level of flexibility and challenge from my work." Approaching work from both a short- and long-range perspective allows you to plan for what you want to do now as well as what you are willing to do in the future. While you might accept one job initially that requires heavier travel commitments and hours, you might want to purposely take a less demanding job as your next career step.

WHAT IS BALANCE FOR YOU?

In order for you to be an authentic leader, you need to bring your whole self to work, including your contributions and your needs. You may be constantly juggling your priorities, but you will get smarter and more adept at doing so as you go along. The key to work/life integration is to be aware of and monitor your satisfaction levels, values, and well-being. Without self-awareness, no amount of work/life benefits or initiatives can make a difference.

Erin McGinnis shared a great image with me when she said, "I visualize my work/life balance like one of those performers balancing many spinning plates. Each plate is different; they could represent your religion, health, job, finances, or family life. I know that it's only a couple times a year that all my plates are spinning at the same time, and when that happens, it's likely that one plate will fall off. When that happens, I know I'll need to spend time rebalancing my plates during those times until I reach equilibrium again." Similarly, Lora J. Villarreal, Ph.D., Executive Vice President and Chief People Officer at Affiliated Computer Services, Inc. (ACS), noted, "To be a leader, you have to actively manage four things: community, spirituality, work, and family. When one of those areas is off kilter, you need to rebalance them. Sometimes it's natural to give one area more of your attention for a while, but it's all about keeping those four areas in check." What buckets of your life are most important? Keep those in mind as you calibrate your sense of balance. As you can see from the words of these leaders, the most important "project" you can manage is you.

9

THINKING WITH THE END IN MIND

AVOID CAREER MYOPIA

As you think about your career, consider the long-term goals, experiences, and positions you would like to have. Rather than imposing barriers on yourself, such as, "I could never make that much money" or "I'd have to be a financial whiz to do that job," dwell instead on what is possible. Strategizing in a long-term way can help you start to build a bridge *now* that can connect you to the destination where you ultimately want to be. Karen Holbrook, Ph.D., Vice President of Research and Innovation at University of South Florida and immediate past president of Ohio State University, successfully used this strategy herself. She advised, "You may want to position yourself for your next job if you are considering moving up in your career. When I became a vice chairman, I positioned myself to be an associate dean of the medical school. When that position opened, I wrote to the dean personally telling him why I was the right candidate. When I wanted to be a president, I filled holes in my résumé by first taking a job as a provost. Always think ahead to your next career step."

What kind of return are you getting from the investment you are making in your current role? Do you get back as much, the same, or less than you are giving your employer? Whatever the case may be, try to fit your current role into a larger, thought-out career strategy. Kelly Pickett, a senior manager at a management consulting firm, recalled one of the strategic career moves she made, noting, "The best advice I got was from a woman [who] hired me early in my career. The job was slightly below my level but it was part of a larger strategy for me to get into an important company. The woman who ultimately hired me knew that the job likely wouldn't challenge me for very long and she said to me, 'If you are still in this job in two years, I'll fire you.' The main advice here is if you're using a job as some kind of stepping stone, make sure it pays off. You need to remember to move on." Taking a long-range view can help you ward off short-term or narrow thinking. Reminding yourself of your long-term goals keeps you focused on your end destination, even if you take a few detours along the way.

YOUR FUTURE SUCCESSES

Is there a particular role you have dreamed of having or a company you would love to work for? Take some time to think about what experiences you would like listed on your résumé in the future. Below are some examples of accomplishments to help you generate your own list:

- Give a keynote speech
- Attain a director-level (or higher) role at a company
- Accept an international work assignment
- Deliver a seminar or training session in an area of my strength
- Launch my own company
- Go to graduate school
- Operationalize (from scratch) a concept I come up with
- Publish an article/book/paper
- Apply for and get a grant
- Make a salary of $_____

To avoid career myopia, you need to employ a forward-looking strategy to attain your leadership goals. What is on your list of future successes? What patterns do you notice looking at your list? Doing this simple exercise from time to time can help guide you toward better, more satisfying work choices.

A HEALTHY TOLERANCE FOR RISK

Ultimately your path to leadership should reflect the strategy that resonates best with you. I firmly believe that the "career ladder" of the past looks more like a "career lattice" today, where people can move in a way that is zigzagged or linear, fast or slow, multifaceted or extremely focused. Patricia Deyton, Director of the Center for Gender in Organizations at Simmons School of Management, explained that, "There are many avenues for moving up; not one. Women need to look at the opportunities presented to them and be willing to stretch. You don't always want to stay with what's comfortable." Accepting a level of risk is required if you are going to move into roles with increasing levels of responsibility. Moreover, an organization's culture and tolerance to risk evolve through stories of times when people took a chance on a project, person, or idea. The way is which an organization accepts risk can serve to encourage or discourage more of it. Regardless of where you work, if you are going to become a leader—or grow—you will need to accept that risk is part of the job.

In the case of Donna Callejon, Chief Operating Officer at Global-Giving, not all career moves she made were upward or vertical. Donna shared, "I'm a calculated risk-taker. When I was 24, I moved from California to Washington, DC, for a lateral job. Some people might not take a risk like that for a lateral job, but I did; and the rest is history." In Donna's case, her history is an impressive one. She went on to become the youngest senior executive in the history of Fannie Mae, and then took a role as GlobalGiving's Chief Operating Officer. Most job opportunities, lateral or vertical, are as fruitful as you make them. If you see a lateral opportunity that excites you and fits into your career strategy, it could broaden your skills and widen your exposure to future promotion opportunities.

Promotions, as exciting as they are, tend come with some anxiety. Unless we have been doing the exact job we are getting promoted into, the unknown aspects of a higher-ranking job can be daunting at first. Consider the example of Catherine J. Mathis, Senior Vice President of Corporate Communications at The New York Times Company. She told me, "When I first took over as a vice president, I felt completely overwhelmed. Taking the job felt like a big risk. There were so many new areas to manage, but I took a cue from others who thought I could do the job. That, in part, gave me confidence to think that I could succeed." If there is a risk you need to take and your confidence falters, whom can you turn to for encouragement? Identify who your go-to advisors and cheerleaders are and seek their counsel when you need your faith restored.

SEIZING OPPORTUNITIES

Are there job opportunities that you have shied away from in the past? Have you declined an interesting assignment, job, or project because of the risk involved? The executives I interviewed credited taking career gambles and making geographic moves as having helped their ascension to leadership. For example, Vicki Ho, General Manager, Asia Services for GE Healthcare Clinical Services at General Electric, noted, "You will always be competing against other risk takers, so you need to take risks, too. I moved my husband to China for my job, which was a huge risk. . . . If you get a wild job offer, take it or someone else will. Some women define their boundaries too much, but you need to be agile. The company is not there to make you successful—that is your job." We can often talk ourselves into the notion that we need "one more job" before we will be ready for a new opportunity. If others believe in you enough to offer you such a role, you may want to heed their confidence in you and discard your self doubts.

Carla E. Lucchino, Assistant Deputy Commandant, Installations and Logistics at the U.S. Marine Corps, had similar advice. In Carla's impressive career, she was promoted at the age of 39 to the Senior Executive Service, the highest one can climb in the federal government. Carla advised, "Seize opportunities and don't be afraid of new challenges. I was once offered a human resources job, took 24 hours to think about it; and in the time I was considering the opportunity, someone else took the job."

TAKING THE LEAP ABROAD

One seemingly risky and yet exciting career move you can make is to seek out an international work opportunity. As Cathy Fleming, Partner at Nixon Peabody LLP, noted, "If you want to be the top person in your area, you may have to make sacrifices such as moving to another state or country for a period." International opportunities can involve short-term business travel, a job rotation, or assignments that are indefinite in length. Whatever the job configuration, international assignments can broaden you personally and professionally, increase your compensation, and lead to significant responsibility and promotion opportunities.

In their thought-provoking book, *Get Ahead by Going Abroad: A Woman's Guide to Fast-Track Career Success,* C. Perry Yeatman and Stacie Nevadomski Berdan make a compelling argument for the fact that taking assignments abroad can fast-track a woman's career. In a survey they conducted for the book, the authors found that:

- 85% agreed international experience accelerated their careers
- 78% agreed that it had a significant, positive impact on compensation
- 71% agreed they were given greater responsibility earlier on
- 53% agreed that an international experience is one of the best ways to break through the glass ceiling (Yeatman & Berdan, 2007)

If your boss approaches you about an international assignment, consider the affect it could have on your total career. Many international assignments are known for being hands-on opportunities, in which people are given more responsibility than they might receive in their home location. While there are certainly risks involved, weigh them thoughtfully and fully consider the rewards as well. Any way that you can build your cultural competence, particularly in the global economy, will serve you on the job.

CORPORATE AMERICA IS NOT FOR EVERYONE

Despite the strategies aspiring leaders can use to thrive in the business world, many women feel a mismatch with corporate America that propels them to leave. There are many theories as to why decreasing numbers of women stay in the full-time workforce. One reason is cited by Vicki Ho, who shared, "Many women choose not to stay in the corporate world because they don't have an appetite for organizational politics. These politics get worse the further up the ladder one goes." Certainly a negative work culture could lead to women seeing corporate America unfavorably. Considerable research, however, has been done to highlight the exact reasons why women make the often difficult decision to leave the workplace.

One such global study of women managers in multinational companies was commissioned by Dell and carried out by Harris Interactive in 2005. The findings of this study showed that the top three reasons that women leave the workforce were: (1) personal/family obligations (79%), (2) excessive work hours that hindered women's abilities to meet familial obligations (73%), and (3) a personal choice to stay home to be a wife or mother (67%). Interestingly, when results were segmented by region, American women by far listed excessive work hours as the reason for leaving (81% versus 63% for Asian women and 71% for European women; 55% of the Latin American women found work hours excessive) (Rudrappa, 2005). When women leave the workplace, regardless of the reason, companies and society as a whole suffer from a less diverse, inclusive workforce. Ultimately, women need to make their own personal decisions about whether or not they can be accommodated in the corporate work world.

BREAKING OUT ON YOUR OWN

Increasingly, women who leave corporate America are considering embarking on their own career paths as entrepreneurs. While the majority of this book applies to individuals employed by a business, nonprofit organization, or government body, it is important to dedicate some time to entrepreneurship as a possible path to leadership. Starting your own business, while a career risk, is also an endeavor in which women can see major rewards.

If you have ever considered starting a business, I encourage you to explore what it would take to do so. Many people opt out of their dream careers before they have even researched them or investigated what it would take to launch them. In the following section, I outline for you the most critical characteristics of entrepreneurs and important considerations in starting your own business.

THE MAKEUP OF AN ENTREPRENEUR

Many people and organizations have researched the traits of successful entrepreneurs. Studying the common traits among entrepreneurs gives you a sense of what keeps them successful and resilient. The characteristics presented below by no means exclude other traits, but tell you instead what many top entrepreneurs have in common:

- **Raw Talent**—As an entrepreneur, you need to know where you have raw talent and intelligence that exceeds that of others. Is it in your financial acumen? Is it your ingenious product? Is it based on the fact that you can present or sell your socks off? Being aware of your smarts and levering them will serve you and your business.
- **Competitive Advantage**—What about your offering or product fills an unmet need? What about your product attracts customers in ways that other firms' offerings have faltered? Once you know the answers to these questions and can ensure that you have a unique or needed offering, you can best position it.
- **Optimism**—Most important, entrepreneurs tend to have a confident, optimistic attitude. If not, how else would they take the financial and other gambles that they do? Commenting on this topic was Mei Xu, Founder and Chief Executive Officer of Chesapeake Bay Candle, Blissliving Home. Mei reflected, "Entrepreneurs are a special species. . . . Entrepreneurs have an overly optimistic attitude, which you really need in order to thrive. Our optimism is not about blind faith; it is about overcoming obstacles."
- **Tolerance for Risk**—A critical characteristic of an entrepreneur, having a tolerance for and even embracing risk is important. There are no guarantees in entrepreneurship, so a business owner must assume risks almost every day.
- **Passion**—A requirement of entrepreneurship, having enthusiasm and interest in your business is necessary. Having real passion for

your service, product, or business offering helps give you drive and longevity.

- **Leadership**—Clearly, entrepreneurship requires leadership abilities since you are the one in charge. To thrive as an entrepreneur, you must be able to guide, inspire, influence, and direct others. These people may be employees, partners, customers, or other stakeholders.

In the article "Five Traits of Successful Entrepreneurs," featured in *Inc.* magazine online, Walter G. Kortschak, a well-regarded and highly experienced venture capitalist, wrote about important leadership characteristics. He outlined traits of successful business owners, gleaned from evaluating hundreds of entrepreneurs both from investment and shareholder standpoints. One of the criteria Kortschak looks for is leaders with the ability to make strategic decisions based on limited data. Since entrepreneurs do not often have the luxury of having all the information needed for a decision, those who can continually make decisions with only partial information succeed (2007). Carla Lucchino reinforced this point when she said, "I like risk. I often have to make quick decisions with 20 percent of the relevant information. If I take a risk and it doesn't work out, I always try to learn from it."

Kortschak also pointed out that successful entrepreneurs learn from their mistakes. Setbacks, while not uncommon in self-employment, are incredibly important to learn from. Having an honest view of your own weaknesses is a critical trait of entrepreneurs, according to Kortschak, since most entrepreneurs do not have deep expertise in all of the subjects they need to manage. Kortschak noted that, "The best entrepreneurs understand this, however, and hire experts who can complement their skills" (2007).

According to Kortschak, an entrepreneur also needs to be able to see patterns, separate key data, and pinpoint the most critical aspects of it. Lastly, partnering successfully with others differentiates the best entrepreneurs. A significant amount of entrepreneurship is based on cultivating and maintaining relationships. Not only just with the customers one serves, but also with employees, vendors, partners, investors, and service providers (2007).

CONSIDERATIONS IN STARTING YOUR OWN BUSINESS

As you consider entrepreneurship and the risks inherent to it, keep an open mind. In Table 9.1, I present some of the most compelling factors, positive and negative, to be aware of in starting a business.

Table 9.1   Positive and Negative Considerations in Owning Your Own Business

Positive Considerations	Negative Considerations
Financial gains, unlimited income potential, perception that you are paid what you are worth	Financial risks, upfront investments, unstable income stream, more liabilities
Flexibility in schedule, working on your own terms	Long hours, potential of a 24/7 operation
You are in control, Chief "Decision" Officer	Isolation, lack of support
You own your successes 100 percent	You own your problems/ failures 100 percent
Creative freedom to execute your vision	Uncertainty, lack of structure
Prestige of owning your own business, greater job satisfaction	No task can be too lowly to do yourself

There are numerous resources available to guide new business owners and encourage women's participation in entrepreneurship. Some of these include:

- The U.S. Small Business Administration (SBA)—The SBA is an independent federal government agency that provides numerous free tools and skilled counsel to help the interests of small business owners (SBA, n.d.).
- SCORE—SCORE, "Counselors to America's Small Business," is a nonprofit association dedicated to educating entrepreneurs and the formation, growth, and success of small business nationwide. SCORE is a resource partner of the SBA and offers many free resources. They have helped businesses such as Vermont Teddy Bear, Vera Bradley Designs, and Jelly Belly Candy (SCORE, n.d.).
- The U.S. Women's Chamber of Commerce (USWCC)—The USWCC is a membership organization that creates economic and leadership opportunities for women through networking and advocacy. USWCC helps members learn and select the best business and financial solutions to increase economic opportunities and offers networking events, information, and resources for business owners (USWCC, n.d.).
- StartupNation— This Web site provides useful, free advice and was founded "*by* entrepreneurs *for* entrepreneurs." The Web site provides sound online content and counsel, and fosters a supportive community for entrepreneurs (StartupNation, n.d.).

- PartnerUp—Founded in 2005, PartnerUp is the largest online community for small business owners and entrepreneurs. Their mission is to "connect innovators with the people, advice, and resources they need to build and grow their businesses." This Web site allows you to find a business partner or colleague for your business by posting your business idea so that interested parties can connect with you (PartnerUp, n.d.).

Many magazines, books, trainings, coaches, and software also exist to guide the new entrepreneur through the process, where so many have already walked. In addition, some contests geared at first time business owners, and women business owners specifically, offer incentives or seed money to launch a business. One interesting example is the Cartier Women's Initiative Awards, which offers winners of its business plan contest $20,000, media coverage, business coaching support, an invitation to a global women's forum, and access to an influential network of female entrepreneurs (Cartier, Women's Forum, McKinsey & Company, & INSEAD, n.d.).

WHAT DOES IT TAKE TO BE AN ENTREPRENEUR?

Clearly, taking the path of entrepreneurship is a major decision that requires the consultation and support of your personal network. When I asked Barbara A. F. Greene, Chief Executive Officer of Greene and Associates, Inc., for example, what allowed her to be most successful as an entrepreneur, she said, "My husband and his support. He gave me the freedom to grow my business and really make it happen. When I won a huge bid that meant I'd be working long hours, he supported me 100 percent." If you decide to embark on forming your own company, consider whose support you can enlist.

Entrepreneurship is not for everyone, but certainly represents an opportunity for a woman to lead on her own terms. Since so much of entrepreneurship is trial and experimentation, staying resilient is one of the best ways to stay buoyant. Mei Xu told me, "Mentally, you must be prepared to fail, and yet entrepreneurs are far more focused on success than failure. . . . Entrepreneurs need to have the raw talent to succeed, in addition to being in the right place at the right time. The way I see it, an entrepreneur falls ten times for every four times a corporate leader falls. I don't look back or count the times I have fallen; I try to focus on success and on what is ahead."

IS THERE EVER A PERFECT TIME?

Some of us can get seduced into thinking that there will be one particularly good time to focus on our career, start a business, change jobs, go back to school, write a book, or live out our dream. In actuality, there is no such thing as a "perfect time." When you accept that fact, you can be more open to opportunities as they arise, and less bound to a rigid plan.

Interestingly, the leaders I spoke with had a "just do it" mentality when it came to pursuing even their loftiest goals. They considered risks and leaps from different angles, without analyzing their ambitions to death, and then trusted their instincts to act. Naomi C. Earp, Chair of the U.S. Equal Employment Opportunity Commission (EEOC), reiterated this point when she said, "Unless someone is a doctor or engineer—whose risks could have fatal consequences—take risks! Society moves forward because people venture something new, not because they play it safe. Push through your fear and seize new opportunities." The fact is that we will always have multiple priorities, which will continually change throughout our lives. We can plan to the best of our abilities, but we must be open to the spontaneous events in life, which often have a way of intervening in our plans.

MANAGING OTHERS' EXPECTATIONS

Women have high expectations put on them in just about every area of their lives. Along with those expectations—and perhaps due to them—comes our desire to accommodate others' needs. As hard as it may be, you have to let others' expectations of you fall away. It is truly up to you to decide what excites you and to go for it. Kelly Pickett reminds us of what is important. She shared, "You're only successful if you value what you do. Even if the whole world thinks you should take one particularly coveted path, it means nothing unless you're happy with it. I think it's easier to be promotable than it is to be successful. Success implies that you have found some meaning in your work and actually enjoy it." There are perils of taking a job based solely on others' hopes for you, or based on prestige alone, one of which is that it will not bring you lasting career satisfaction.

AUTHENTICALLY YOU

In this book, you have been presented with many strategies for getting to and succeeding at leadership. My interviews have illustrated how other women have achieved leadership status, and what you can learn from their successes, risks, and failures. Ultimately, however, you have to take your unique abilities and strengths into account and decide what kind of leadership voice you have.

Vicki Ho talked about being authentic, referencing femininity and masculinity. She noted, "One challenge that plagues women leaders is in how feminine or masculine to be. Women want to be tough without being tagged with the 'b word.' A lot of women who fight to move up in a company end up behaving like men—an example is the commentary made about Hillary Clinton. She only seems to score with the public when she's being softer and more genuine than her usual self." As long as you come from a place of authenticity in leadership, even your failures will be safeguarded from deep-seated regret. It is only when you try to be someone you are not that you will face significant internal conflict. Mei Xu shared a different vision, noting, "I like to think that as women business leaders we can be feminine and beautiful, as well as strong and powerful. Don't be afraid of your femininity or your power. You can combine both. And if anyone has a problem with it, it is their problem, not yours."

One of the most compelling stories about being authentic comes from Maya Rockeymoore, Ph.D., President and Founder of Global Policy Solutions. She recounted, "My graduate school experience was very male-dominated and was the ultimate test in being taken seriously. Professors assumed you weren't serious if you took the time to curl your hair or paint your fingernails. . . . Later I tried to make people take me more seriously at work by being more serious. I did this until one day a colleague surprised me by asking me why I never smiled. Now I don't try to assert habits or traits, I just try to be who I am. I speak out assertively about things that are important, I show my dedication and creativity, and I strive to be respectful of others." Wearing a mask, even if you do it convincingly, will never give you a deep sense of well-being or satisfaction. I encourage you to find your own leadership style, speak out, and share your message authentically.

WHAT KIND OF LEGACY WILL YOU LEAVE?

Synchronizing your work and personal selves means thinking career-wide—not just job-to-job. Positioning yourself for leadership requires you to go into new job situations with the end in mind. How do you want to be remembered on the job? What kind of legacy will you leave at your workplace? As your career targets continue to shift and move, you will need to keep reflecting on where your most deeply held values lie. As you grow and succeed, I encourage you to pull others up with you. Madeline Albright, the first woman to become United States Secretary of State, is quoted as having once said, "There is a special place in hell for women who don't help other women." Think about how, as you achieve leadership success, you can help others who are not there yet.

When I interviewed the 30 women executives, I was surprised and interested to hear responses to the interview question, "What would you like your career legacy to be?" While I expected many answers to relate to starting a new division, being a business visionary, or being the first women to blaze a trail in a male-dominated area, what I heard was different. Most of all, the women I interviewed wanted to be seen as positive role models that developed and taught others. Below are some representative examples from the interviews:

Sample responses to, "What would you like your career legacy to be?"

- "I hope my legacy is that I created and unlocked a different type of leader. I want to be remembered for helping people to find their passion in life and aligning it with their work." –Melissa M. Monk, Chief Infrastructure Officer at Capital One
- "Professionally, I'd like to be remembered for doing something unprecedented. Personally, I'd like my legacy to be that I was someone people liked working for." –Erin McGinnis, National Committee Chair of the Society of Women Engineers
- "If I am remembered as successful in my career, I'd like it to be because of the women's leadership work I've done. If I created more opportunities for women to lead, then I will be happy." –DeeDee Wilson, Chief Financial Officer at Aritzia
- "That I tried to help people." –Naomi C. Earp, Chair of the U.S. Equal Employment Opportunity Commission (EEOC)
- "That I did good things for people and the world, even if only in my small circle. Also that my husband and kids are proud of me." –Rosslyn Kleeman, Chair of the Coalition for Effective Change
- "I'd want my legacy to be that I hired good people to support me, that I gave them the growth opportunities that they wanted, and took the time to help young people starting out in their careers. I'd like to be remembered as a mentor and someone who is kind." –D'Arcy Foster Rudnay, Senior Vice President for Comcast Corporation

How will people describe you after you leave your organization?

FEAR REGRET MORE THAN FAILURE

If you talk to your elders about regrets, they will most often tell you that they regret the things they did not do more than they regret the things they did do. As you advance your career, I encourage you to approach opportunities with an open mind more than you listen to your fears. Shannon S. S. Herzfeld, Vice President of Government Relations at Archer Daniels Midland Company, advised, "The most significant barrier a woman faces is going into the workplace with the assumption that she'll have to limit her life choices. . . . Looking at my own experience, I took on a lot but didn't compromise a lot." Go find the life you want!

Appendix

INTERVIEW PROTOCOL

This book is the culmination of 30 interviews conducted with a far-reaching group of executive women from corporate, nonprofit, and government sectors. Over the course of a year, I conducted the interviews either in-person or via telephone, transcribing the interview material verbatim. Once all of the interview transcriptions were recorded, I performed a qualitative data analysis to analyze trends and synthesize overarching themes. The dominant themes from the interviews serve as the foundation for chapters 2–9 of this book.

INTERVIEW QUESTIONS

The interview protocol included the following questions:

- What are the main barriers that young women face in advancing their careers?
- What advantages are in a young woman's favor?
- What particular competencies or skills have made you promotable?
- What do you consider the most valuable training a Generation X or Y woman can receive?
- What importance do you feel networking plays for women just starting out? If networking is important, what types of networks or groups?
- What role does self-reflection play in moving up professionally?

- How would you recommend that young women get a good grasp of their strengths and weaknesses?
- What kind of advice would you give a woman just entering the workplace?
- Are there any outside activities that can supplement a young woman's portfolio and improve her performance at work?
- Have you personally sought out formal mentors in the past? How was that experience for you?
- What has allowed you to be most successful at work?
- Have any traits served you particularly well at navigating office politics?
- Do you always listen to your instincts or do you challenge them? Why or why not?
- How much of a role has persistence played in helping you move up the corporate/nonprofit/government ladder?
- Can a young woman say "no" at work and still expect to move up?
- What traits or habits have helped you to be taken seriously at work?
- What are you most proud of professionally?
- What piece of advice has stayed with you most over the years?
- Tell me about a woman leader that you look up to.
- How do you approach work/life balance? How would you advise a new leader to approach work/life balance?
- What strategy for advancing one's career goes overlooked most?
- Tell me a story about an experience that prepared you well for your management/leadership position.
- What skills do you credit in helping you become a leader? How important are technical versus "soft" skills?
- Do you recommend that women who want to lead become specialists in their field or generalists?
- What is your approach to risk taking? Tell me about a career risk you took.
- What do you wish you had known at the beginning of your career?
- What was your best career moment?
- What would you like your career legacy to be?

WOMEN LEADERS PROFILED

The following list represents the women I interviewed for this book.

Katharine Weymouth, Publisher of the *Washington Post* and Chief Executive Officer of Washington Post Media

Cynthia Egan, President of Retirement Plan Services at T. Rowe Price

D'Arcy Foster Rudnay, Senior Vice President for Comcast Corporation

Lora J. Villarreal, Ph.D., Executive Vice President and Chief People Officer at Affiliated Computer Services, Inc. (ACS)

Naomi C. Earp, Chair of the U.S. Equal Employment Opportunity Commission (EEOC)

Barbara A. F. Greene, Chief Executive Officer of Greene and Associates, Inc.

Patricia Deyton, Director of the Center for Gender in Organizations at Simmons School of Management

Donna Callejon, Chief Operating Officer at GlobalGiving

Karen Holbrook, Ph.D., Vice President of Research and Innovation at University of South Florida, and immediate past president of Ohio State University

Maya Rockeymoore, Ph.D., President and Founder of Global Policy Solutions

Cuc T. Vu, Chief Diversity Officer at Human Rights Campaign

Alexandra Miller, Chief Executive Officer of Mercedes Medical, Inc.

Erin McGinnis, National Committee Chair of the Society of Women Engineers

Autumn Bayles, Senior Vice President, Strategic Operations at Tasty Baking Company

Courteney Monroe, Executive Vice President of Consumer Marketing at HBO

Dominique Schurman, Chief Executive Officer of Papyrus

Vicki Ho, General Manager, Asia Services for GE Healthcare Clinical Services at General Electric

Melissa M. Monk, Chief Infrastructure Officer at Capital One

Kelly Pickett, senior manager at a management consulting firm

DeeDee Wilson, Chief Financial Officer at Aritzia

Rosslyn Kleeman, Chair of the Coalition for Effective Change

Cathy Fleming, Partner at Nixon Peabody LLP

Carla E. Lucchino, Assistant Deputy Commandant, Installations and Logistics at the U.S. Marine Corps

Roxanne Spillett, President and CEO of Boy and Girls Clubs of America

Jeanine Becker, Senior Counsel at Motorola, Inc.

Catherine J. Mathis, Senior Vice President of Corporate Communications at The New York Times Company

Shannon S. S. Herzfeld, Vice President of Government Relations at Archer Daniels Midland Company

Denise Incandela, President of Saks Direct at Saks Fifth Avenue

Jamie McCourt, President of the Los Angeles Dodgers

Mei Xu, Founder and Chief Executive Officer of Chesapeake Bay Candle, Blissliving Home

BIBLIOGRAPHY

CHAPTER 1

American Psychological Association. (1999). Employees perceive women as better managers, study finds. *APA Monitor Online, 30*(8). Retrieved May 1, 2009, from http://www.apa.org/monitor/sep99/nl2.html

Catalyst. (2005). Catalyst Census of Women Board Directors of the Fortune 500 Shows 10-Year Trend of Slow Progress and Persistent Challenges. Retrieved May 1, 2009, from http://www.catalyst.org/press-release/90/2005-catalyst-census-of -women-board-directors-of-the-fortune-500-shows-10-year-trend-of-slow -progress-and-persistent-challenges

Catalyst. (2008). Catalyst Census of Women Corporate Officers and Top Earners of the Fortune 500, Research Reports. Published: December 2008. Updated on January 12, 2009. Retrieved July 21, 2009, from http://www.catalyst.org/ publication/283/2008-catalyst-census-of-women-corporate-officers-and-top -earners-of-the-fortune-500

Catalyst. (2009). *Catalyst Pyramids: U.S. Women in Business.* Retrieved May 1, 2009, from http://www.catalyst.org/publication/132/us-women-in-business

Catalyst. (2009). *Women in Law, Quick Takes.* Retrieved May 1, 2009, from http://www.catalyst.org/file/208/qt_women_in_law.pdf

DeGroat, T. J. (2006). *No Way to Measure Diversity's Value? Mainstream Article Ignores the Hard Facts.* Retrieved May 1, 2009, from http://www .diversityinc.com

Institute for Women's Policy Research. (2008). The Gender Wage Gap: 2008 Fact Sheet. Retrieved May 1, 2009, from http://www.iwpr.org/pdf/C350.pdf

Merrill Lynch. (2005). *When It Comes to Investing, Gender a Strong Influence on Behavior.* As Investors, Women Less Knowledgeable and Interested than Men, But Make Fewer Mistakes (And Don't Repeat Them as Often). Merrill Lynch Investment Managers (MLIM). Retrieved May 1, 2009, from http://www.ml.com/media/47547.pdf

Moore, M., & Trahan R. (1997). Biased and Political: Student Perceptions of Females Teaching About Gender, *College Student Journal, 31*(4) 434–444.

National Center for Education Statistics. (2007). Digest of Education Statistics, "Table 269: First-professional degrees conferred by degree-granting institutions in dentistry, medicine, and law, by number of institutions conferring degrees and sex of student: Selected years, 1949–50 through 2005–06" and "Table 264: Bachelor's, master's, and doctor's degrees conferred by degree-granting institutions, by field of study and year: Selected years, 1970–71 through 2005–06."

National Women's Law Center. (n.d.). The Fair Pay Campaign: Working for Fair Pay for All. Retrieved May 1, 2009, from http://www.nwlc.org/fairpay/

Open Congress. (2009). Lilly Ledbetter Fair Pay Act of 2009. Retrieved May 1, 2009, from http://www.opencongress.org/bill/111-s181/show

Peters, T. (2006). *Re-Imagine! Business Excellence in a Disruptive Age.* New York: DK Publishing, Inc.

Phelan, J. E., Moss-Racusin, C. A., & Rudman, L. A. (2008). Competent Yet Out in the Cold: Shifting Criteria for Hiring Reflect Backlash Toward Agentic Women, Rutgers University–New Brunswick, *Psychology of Women Quarterly, 32*(4), 406–413. American Psychological Association.

Rosener, J. B. (1997). *America's Competitive Secret: Women Managers.* New York: Oxford University Press.

Shellenbarger, S. (2008). *The Mommy M.B.A.: Schools Try to Attract More Women.* Retrieved July 21, 2009, from http://online.wsj.com/article/SB121918306439554611.html

U.S. Equal Employment Opportunity Commission. (1963, modified 2009). The Equal Pay Act of 1963. Retrieved May 1, 2009, from http://www.eeoc.gov/policy/epa.html

WAGE. (n.d.). The WAGE Project. Retrieved May 1, 2009, from http://www.wageproject.org

CHAPTER 2

Career Coach Institute. (n.d.). Retrieved May 1, 2009, from http://www.careercoachinstitute.com

Gallup. (2006). Gallup Study: Engaged Employees Inspire Company Innovation. *Gallup Management Journal.*

Mitchell, C. and H. Coltrinari. (2001). *Journal Writing for Teachers and Students, The Craft of Teaching Adults,* 3rd ed., edited by T. Barer-Stein and M. Kompf. Toronto, Ontario: Irwin Publishing.

National Career Development Association (NCDA). (n.d.). Retrieved May 1, 2009, from http://www.NCDA.org

The Riley Guide: Self-Assessment Resources. (2009). Retrieved July 6, 2009, from http://www.rileyguide.com/assess.html

Robinson, D., Perryman, S., & Hayday, S. (2004). *The Drivers of Employee Engagement,* Institute for Employment Studies, Report 408. Retrieved May 1, 2009, from http://www.employment-studies.co.uk/pubs/summary.php?id=408

U.S. Securities and Exchange Commission (SEC). (2009). Form 10-K. Retrieved May 1, 2009, from http://www.sec.gov/answers/form10k.htm

CHAPTER 3

Carnegie, D. (1982). *How to Win Friends and Influence People* (rev. ed.). New York: Simon and Schuster.

Glaser, C. (2007). *GenderTalk Works: 7 Steps for Cracking the Gender Code at Work.* New York: Windsor Hall.

Hyde, J., Lindberg, S., Linn, M., Ellis, A., & Williams, C. (2008). Gender Similarities Characterize Math Performance. *Science, 321*(5888), 494–495.

Kouzes, J. M., & Posner, B. Z. (2007). *The Leadership Challenge,* 4th ed. San Francisco: Jossey-Bass.

Mehrabian, A. (1971). *Silent Messages.* Belmont, CA: Wadsworth.

Sadker, M., & Sadker, D. (1995). *Failing at Fairness: How Our Schools Cheat Girls.* New York: Touchstone.

Winerman, L. (2005). Men receive more credit than women for joint work on stereotypically male tasks. *Monitor on Psychology, American Psychological Association 36*(11), 11. Retrieved May 1, 2009, from http://www.apa.org/monitor/dec05/tasks.html

CHAPTER 4

Accenture. (2008). *One Step Ahead of 2011: A New Horizon for Working Women.* Retrieved May 1, 2009, from https://microsite.accenture.com/NonSecureSiteCollectionDocuments/By_Subject/Strategy/PDF/IWD Research_final.pdf

Peters, T. (1997). The Brand Called You. *Fast Company, 10.* Retrieved May 1, 2009, from http://www.fastcompany.com/magazine/10/brandyou.html

CHAPTER 5

Frost, J., & McKelvie, S. J. (2005). The Relationship of Self-Esteem and Body Satisfaction to Exercise Activity for Male and Female Elementary School, High School, and University Students. Department of Psychology, Bishop's University. *Athletic Insight, 7*(4). Retrieved May 1, 2009, from http://www.athleticinsight.com/Vol7Iss4/Selfesteem.htm

Graduate Management Admission Council® (GMAC®). (2008). The MBA Alumni Perspectives Survey. Retrieved May 1, 2009, from http://www.gmac.com/NR/rdonlyres/9EEEEA50-4747-409A-B5C0-88E24135DEC5/0/MBAAlumniPerspectivesSurveyReport2008.pdf

CHAPTER 6

Babcock, L., & Laschever, S. (2003). *Women Don't Ask: Negotiation and the Gender Divide.* Princeton, N.J.: Princeton University Press.

Institute for Women's Policy Research (IWPR). (2009). IWPR Publication #C350: The Gender Wage Gap: 2008. Retrieved May 1, 2009, from http://www.iwpr.org/pdf/C350.pdf

Small, D. A., Gelfand, M., Babcock, L., & Gettman, H. (2005). Who Goes to the Bargaining Table? Understanding Gender Variation in the Initiation of Negotiations. Center for Behavioral Decision Research at Carnegie Mellon University. Retrieved May 1, 2009, from http://www.cbdr.cmu.edu/papers/pdfs/cdr_090.pdf

The Wage Project, Inc. (n.d.). What Are the Costs of the Wage Gap? Retrieved May 1, 2009, from http://www.wageproject.org/content/gap/costs.php

CHAPTER 7

Bacharach, S. B. (2005). *Get Them on Your Side.* Avon, MA: Platinum Press.

Goleman, D. (1998). *Working with Emotional Intelligence.* New York: Bantam Books.

International Network for Social Network Analysis (INSNA). (2008). Retrieved May 1, 2009, from http://www.insna.org

Sanders, T. (2006). *The Likeability Factor: How to Boost Your L-Factor and Achieve Your Life's Dreams.* New York: Random House.

Schein, E. (2004). *Organizational Culture and Leadership.* San Francisco: Jossey-Bass.

CHAPTER 8

Bailyn, L., Drago, R., & Kochan, T. A. (2001). Integrating Work and Family Life: A Holistic Approach. Report of the Sloan Work-Family Policy Network. MIT Sloan School of Management.

CNN.com. (2001). Transcripts. Larry King Live. What's Next for Martha Stewart? Aired February 2, 2001, 9:00 p.m. ET. Retrieved May 1, 2009, from http://transcripts.cnn.com/TRANSCRIPTS/0102/02/lkl.00.html

Fortune Magazine. (2009). 100 Best Companies to Work For®. Retrieved May 1, 2009, from http://www.greatplacetowork.com/best/100best-2009/100best-2009-list.php

Hewlett, S. A., & Luce, C. B. (2006). Extreme Jobs: The Dangerous Allure of the 70-Hour Workweek. *Harvard Business Review, 84*(12), 49–59.

Hewlett, S. A., & Luce, C. B. (2007). Extreme Jobs: The Dangerous Allure of the 70-Hour Workweek. *Harvard Business Review, 85*(4), 136.

Heymann, J., Earle, A., & Hayes, J. (2007). The Work, Family, and Equity Index: How Does the United States Measure Up? The Institute for Health and Social Policy at McGill University. Retrieved May 1, 2009, from http://www.mcgill.ca/files/ihsp/WFEIFinal2007.pdf

McGrath, M., Driscoll, M., & Gross, M. (2005). BACK IN THE GAME. Returning to Business after a Hiatus: Experiences and Recommendations for Women, Employers, and Universities. Wharton Center for Leadership and Change and the Forté Foundation. Retrieved May 1, 2009, from http://knowledge.wharton.upenn.edu/papers/1298.pdf

Pruchno, R., Litchfield, L., & Fried, M. (2000). Measuring the Impact of Workplace Flexibility. Boston College, Center for Work & Family, Wallace E. Carroll School of Management.

Stoner, C. R., & Robin, J. (2006). *A Life in Balance: Finding Meaning in a Chaotic World*. Lanham, MD: University Press of America.

U.S. Department of Labor. (1993). Family and Medical Leave Act of 1993. Retrieved May 1, 2009, from http://www.dol.gov/esa/whd/regs/statutes/fmla.htm

Working Mother Magazine. (2008). 2008 100 Best Companies. Retrieved May 1, 2009, from http://workingmother.com/?service=vpage/109

CHAPTER 9

Cartier, Women's Forum, McKinsey & Company, & INSEAD. (n.d.). The Cartier Women's Initiative Awards. What Can You Win? Retrieved May 1, 2009, from http://www.cartierwomensinitiative.com

Kortschak, W. G. (2007). Five Traits of Successful Entrepreneurs. *Inc.* magazine online. Retrieved May 1, 2009, from http://www.inc.com/inc5000/articles/20070901/kortschak.html

PartnerUp. (n.d.). How It Works. Retrieved May 1, 2009, from http://partnerup.com/howitworks/default.aspx

Rudrappa, S. (2005). Women in a Global Workforce. The University of Texas at Austin, Center for Women's and Gender Studies. Retrieved May 1, 2009, from http://www.dell.com/downloads/global/corporate/press/20050419_ut_whitepaper.pdf

SCORE. (n.d.). About SCORE. Retrieved May 1, 2009, from http://www.score.org/explore_score.html

StartupNation. (n.d.). About StartupNation. Retrieved May 1, 2009, from http://www.startupnation.com

U.S. Small Business Administration (SBA). (n.d.). About the U.S. Small Business Administration. Retrieved May 1, 2009, from http://www.sba.gov/aboutsba/index.html

U.S. Women's Chamber of Commerce (USWCC). (n.d.). About the U.S. Women's Chamber of Commerce. Retrieved May 1, 2009, from http://www.uswcc.org/html/uswcc-about-us.aspx

Yeatman, C. P., & Berdan, S. N. (2007). *Get Ahead by Going Abroad: A Woman's Guide to Fast-Track Career Success*. New York: Collins Living.

INDEX

Note: Page numbers followed by *t* indicate that the reference is to a table on the designated page.

About the Author

Selena Rezvani has guided numerous clients through the process of assessing their workplaces and identifying strategies for transformation. She has consulted widely on issues of organizational change and workforce development, and has worked with varied organizations internationally and across many industries. She provides consulting services that include focus group facilitation, employee opinion surveys, 360-degree assessments, leadership workshops, and career development surveys.

Leveraging her unique combination of business consulting and behavioral science training, Ms. Rezvani's thinking and work are grounded in a multidisciplinary approach. This approach integrates emotional intelligence, strengths-based theory, and an appreciative inquiry perspective. A passion for leveraging others' career potential drives her interests in helping individuals, groups, and organizations achieve results that benefit everyone.

Ms. Rezvani wrote *The Next Generation of Women Leaders* while earning her Master of Business Administration degree from Johns Hopkins University, where she went on to graduate first in her class. She also holds Master of Social Work and Bachelors of Science degrees from New York University. She is active in her favorite non-profit organization, the National Association of Women MBAs, where she serves as a regional vice president and works to propel more women into leadership roles. To learn more about Ms. Rezvani or to contact her, please visit www.nextgenwomen.com.